TWENTIETH–CENTURY SPIRITUAL LETTERS

Books by John B. Coburn

Twentieth-Century Spiritual Letters:
An Introduction to Contemporary Prayer

Anne and the Sand Dobbies

Minister: Man-in-the-Middle

Prayer and Personal Religion
(Layman's Theological Library)

Twentieth-Century
Spiritual Letters

An Introduction to Contemporary Prayer

by
John B. Coburn

The Westminster Press · Philadelphia

PUBLISHED BY THE WESTMINSTER PRESS®
PHILADELPHIA, PENNSYLVANIA

PRINTED IN THE UNITED STATES OF AMERICA

To
My friend
Ruth

CONTENTS

PREFACE

The chapters in this book were originally written as meditations for the Community retreat for the Order of the Holy Cross, an Episcopal religious order for men at West Park, New York, July 25 to August 3, 1966. The framework within which they were originally presented has been changed and much of the material recast for the purposes of the written rather than the spoken word.

Holy Cross has meant much to me for nearly twenty years. During visits to the monastery, and particularly in conversations with the Reverend Alan Whittemore, O.H.C., during the latter years of his life, I have been helped to understand something of the ways of God in dealing with men and been given insight into the mystery of his nature as well as my own. My acceptance of the invitation to conduct the retreat was in response to the Spirit of God that I have known in Father Whittemore and in the Community. In a word, I accepted the invitation as from God, and I have wanted the response to be to him.

Anyway, the only reason I could think of not to accept was cowardice, and that hardly seemed adequate.

This will also enable me to express in print my gratitude to the Father Superior, the Reverend Lincoln A. Taylor, O.H.C., and to the members of the Order of the Holy Cross for the honor of the invitation to share in their retreat and for their cordial hospitality throughout.

I am grateful to my friend and colleague, Prof. Harvey H. Guthrie, Jr., Th.D., who has read the manuscript to help me avoid certain Biblical and theological pitfalls. In some instances, no doubt, he has not been able to rescue me, so I must confess that any heresies that remain are my very own. I also want to express appreciation to my secretary, Mrs. Charles K. Nason, who has typed and retyped this manuscript without losing either her humor or her grace. Both — together with her skill and her sense — have helped immeasurably in completing this assignment.

                                                        J. B. C.

Cambridge, Massachusetts

PART ONE

TWENTIETH–CENTURY SPIRITUAL LETTERS

I

A LETTER TO A SCHOOL FRIEND

Bernardsville, N.J.
December 7, 1935

Dear Coley:

I thought I would try to write you just a note during a wild something I have gotten myself in for, which I thought would never happen to me: a retreat. Do you know what a retreat is?

A retreat is when you go off with six or eight or a dozen other guys, and you have a retreat conductor, and he talks for two days. Everybody else keeps silent. You keep silent. That would be a tough one for you, wouldn't it? And then somebody else usually reads during the meals. The point is that if you go away — beat a retreat, get it? — and withdraw for a while and think about God, then you get straightened out.

The Lord knows I need straightening out, all right, but I do not think this is the way you do it. As a matter of fact, I tried to argue the friend who was pressuring me to come here by saying, " Jack, don't you know that religion is supposed to be a part of life, not apart from it? " I have forgotten who said that, but I thought it was pretty good and would be a real telling blow. He took it in stride, however, and said: " Yes, that's true, but the only way you can get a perspective on how religion can be fully in your life is to step aside every once in a while and take a good, hard look."

Well, I really didn't want to hurt this fellow's feelings. He coached the ends on the football team and was just as nice a guy as you could ever hope for. He takes religion a little too seriously. He thinks everybody understands what the Christian faith is, and all we have to do is just work harder at it. My problem is that I don't even understand what any of the fundamentals are, much less being interested in working at it. Anyway, it really is because he has been such a good friend for three years that I came on this thing.

In between the meditations I'll scribble a few lines to you and bring you up to date. I wish I'd never gotten involved in this thing. Now I'm stuck here for two days. Writing you will at least be a normal thing for me to be doing.

The principal news is that I have broken off with Judy, and now she knows it. I have also broken off with Louise — though she doesn't know it. If I had any guts, I'd tell her, I suppose. Maybe she'll just find out all by herself. That romance goes back a long time — at least three years from that first dance we went to together up at that school in Connecticut. The other news is that I won my varsity letter, which pleases me and gives me a free pass for all next year at the athletic events — and that will help the finances. I have a job and a scholarship, and Dad gives me $400 a year, and I am not about to put myself in any position to ask him for more money.

They have invited somebody named Jones in to talk. He is a very holy fellow, so holy he scares me. I'd hate to have him get his hands on me. He gives a series of meditations. His first one we just had a little while ago, and he didn't say much. He said silence is good because in it we can hear God. That was the first point. The second point is, God says that without vision you die. Animals follow this, he says; fish become frogs. Is that right? Do fish become frogs? Tadpoles become frogs. The third point is, therefore, you've got to look up. So keep looking up. Those three points are supposed to be connected. Read some books and pray. Look up and forget yourself.

Well, that was the first meditation. Now we are sitting around here waiting for the hand of God to give us a slap on the back. The only natural-looking person is a young professor who is here. He is just sitting over there on the other side of the room, peacefully reading a book. Next chance I have I'll go get John Stuart Mill out of my suitcase and get working on him for politics class next week.

One of the students here is sitting stiffly forward on the edge of his chair working like hell to get an inspiration. Another one has been writing furiously ever since the meditation finished. Somebody else is sitting over on the sofa with his hands over his eyes, being very stiff and intent.

I wonder if God is having a good laugh, or is he really impressed? Does this make any difference to him?

It is almost time now for us to go off for a service called "Compline." Once that gets started, we have only thirty-five hours more, and then we'll be free. It will be interesting to see what this Compline turns out to be. I wish I could smoke my pipe, but nobody has made any moves toward smoking yet.

December 8, 1935

Compline, it turned out, wasn't so bad. It was mostly multitudinous responses.

We got up at 6:45 this morning and had Communion.

Old Jones takes charge with a most sepulchral voice. Why does a voice always have to change when the hand of God is around? During breakfast my friend read about a gentleman named Vincent somebody-or-other. I don't know who he was, but the story of him and all the business around here is spooky and unrelated to any stuff I know anything about. Besides that, the damn silence is beginning to get on my nerves.

Last night I thought I'd take old Jones at his word and read one of the books around here. I picked up *Jesus of Nazareth* by Charles Gore. He had a few interesting things to say. One of them is this: "His [Jesus'] refusal to give plain answers to plain questions — his constant habit of dealing with one question by asking another — was, we should gather, part of a general refusal to teach explicitly and dogmatically, lest he should thereby stunt a man's capacity for finding his own answers to his own questions by the light given within him."

This struck me. Why couldn't this be a pretty complete end of life in itself — that is, the asking of questions and each individual guy trying to figure out his answer to the best of his own ability?

As a matter of fact, there is some similarity here with John Stuart Mill and the necessity, he points out, of having a variety of circumstances available if there is ever to be freedom to develop.

Apparently, according to Gore, Jesus recognized a society where there was a hierarchy of orders, but he was dead set against exploitation of the weak and the helpless. At the same time, he didn't make any distinction between sins — that is, selfishness is just as bad as adultery. Or, rather, his distinctions are different. That's news to me. He said that we must look in new directions to restore the supremacy of the spirit over the flesh. I don't know what the devil he means by that. I can't follow it. If he means that the spirit is good and the flesh is bad, I don't think I'll buy it.

Thank the Lord, Coley, I can write to you. The fact is, I could get a lot more out of this whole retreat if I could talk to one or two of these fellows instead of sitting around meditating. I have little enough chance to get their views anyway, and here we go out in the woods and everyone keeps quiet except for the old leader.

Well, now, here we go off again for another — Morning Prayer and Meditation coming up next.

You know what he said? He said that if we're going to have vision, we have to have some sense of sin!!! The trouble with us, he said, is that we're not sorry for our manifold sins and wickedness because we're not Christians. I think that's for the birds. Our mistakes, he says, are sins. Our greatest sins are those we know nothing about. Boy! This guy is crazy. How

can you be sorry for something you don't know anything
about?

Therefore we have to confess. The greatest sin of all, he
says, is forgetfulness of God. When the sense of sin comes,
then we get down on our knees and thank God because we're
on the right track. Boy, I've gotten down on my knees many
times, but I've never gotten down on my knees to thank God
for the sense of sin. I'd like to get rid of that sense of sin.
That's what I keep asking God to let me get out of.

Well, after that we had another interlude, so I read some
more *Jesus of Nazareth*, but didn't get much out of it.

Then there was another meditation in the afternoon.

This one was meant to be on repentance. I must say, my
knees are getting sore, and it's cold as hell in here. I got some
new pipe tobacco — Walnut — it seems to be a lot better than
that Edgeworth. One good thing. Some of these other fellows
are beginning to smoke. That helps.

Repentance, Jones says, isn't just being sorrowful, but must
be a new life. Really, what kind of language is that? He seems
to be a nice guy, but he never gets down to any fundamentals
— like, what makes him think there's a God? How the devil
are we supposed to know there's a God or not? Oh, these talks
are very spiritual and very high up in the air. He then went
on to say that self-centeredness is sin, but that's where we all
are, anyway. We have to have sorrow for the sin we cause —
for the pain we cause. And our trouble is we don't know we
have sin or cause pain. Boy, this is the damndest stuff I've ever
heard. How can you be sorrowful for causing something when
you don't know you're causing it? We can't save ourselves, so
we have to have help from outside, he says — that is, of course,
Christ. Furthermore, we have to worship him to be saved. We
don't want to break our intellects, but we break our hearts by
love. Isn't that neat?

Then he goes on to say that we pray to God to help us. That
seems to be fair enough. Then he says, but that's selfish. So
what in hell are we supposed to be praying for, anyway? Peo-

ple don't pray to help God, but to have God help them. Therefore, all of us are selfish. This is a sin; thus, all our prayers are
sins. Q.E.D.!!! Boy, I think this is the limit.

You might get a lot out of this, Coley, although I don't seem
to be. I tried to get Hank to come. Now, he's a fellow who
would have gotten a good deal out of it. I think he's off the
track. He's a nice guy. He's got as much to offer as anybody
in the world, and his one aim is, he says, " to be respected by
his fellowmen." I don't think that's enough. He refuses to realize that a reputation is just what a guy seems to be; but a
guy's insides are what he really is, and it's the insides that
count.

I feel, I suppose, that somehow I've got a mission in this
world which I'm going to lose myself in one day, and that's
where I'm really going to be in my insides, and that's the only
thing that's going to be important about me. I trust I'll find
out what this is sometime. It sure isn't going to be to follow
my old man.

There's another peculiar thing about this retreat business.
All the other students here are, I guess, nice enough guys, although I only know two or three of them. They certainly
aren't the white-shoe guys. They aren't the average fellows.
They aren't in any clubs, or if they are, I guess some jerky
ones.

What conclusions do you draw from that, Coley, old boy?
Does that mean that you can't be a regular guy and be a Christian, or Christians can't be regular guys, or what? Why is it
that it's the more or less " odd ducks " that are here? Maybe
I'm an odd duck, too. Well, I don't know.

Silence is probably good because I don't have to talk with
these birds and they don't have to talk with me. We probably
wouldn't have much to say to each other, anyway.

We had another meditation at 3:30 this afternoon. " How
do you lead a new life? " old Jonesy asked. He says, you lead
a new life by prayer, the church, and Holy Communion. That
sounds to me as though it came right off the printing press

somewhere. " To be a slave of God is the only way to be free."
You gotta have rules if you're going to do this — that is, if
you're going to be a real slave — and you can break them for
no reason at all, except for the sake of God.

Prayer, he says, is the main thing. But, of course, prayer and
living have got to be entwined. Pray in your spare moments.
Say, " God, I love you." My gosh, isn't that just lovely? What
do you suppose God would do if I should ever just say to him,
" Dear God, I love you "? I might say, " Help me get the hell
out of this jam." He'd fall over flat if he ever heard me say,
" God, I love you." I don't even know if he exists. Anyway,
prayer means that we appreciate something that we get from
God, and he's the source of all good gifts. " Lord," he says,
" do with me what you want — not what I want." I'm not so
sure about that. What have we got our wills for if we can't do
what we want to? Isn't that why we have them?

Anyway, I think this is getting to be too much. The fellow
who was writing so furiously at the beginning just sits now,
and he doesn't look intent about anything. He's done in. The
spirit has gone out. I'm also happy to report that the fire in
the fireplace has finally gotten lighted, and fortunately it
throws out a little heat.

                                                December 9, 1935
The evening meditation last night was pretty simple. He
said the church shouldn't exist for social functions. It has to
be a place of vision where we can meet God. The parish house,
he said, is insidious — the altar is what is important. That's
very hard for me to take. I think the guy doesn't know what
he's talking about. At least he may know what he's talking
about around the altar, but certainly not around the parish
house. You separate from the church, he says, and you die
spiritually. Nuts.

As far as the Communion is concerned, he says, you understand it only after you do it many times. That's a great help,
isn't it?

Now, it's about all over. Let me say a couple of things. I must confess I'm impressed by what apparently is the absolute faith of these two leaders. A great deal of what they say — maybe most of it — I just can't swallow, but I cannot help feeling that these men have hold of something that is vital and real — or vice versa. That is, something has gotten into them, and they're all taken up with it.

The experience, I guess, has been a valuable one, if for no other reason than simply because it brought me out of the collegiate atmosphere for a while with all the junk that goes on there. I fear my spiritual nature is not sufficiently developed to get out of this all that I might. The same end might be reached if only I could decide definitely where the line is between what I want to do and what I can give to society — or, rather, where those lines cross.

Maybe I got a little inkling of this these last two days. Anyway, all the best to you. See you Christmastime. Take care. I'll mail this when I get back to college.

As ever,

A Postscript

Jesus, it took a long time, but now I can see that it was your Spirit at work on that football field that began a human friendship which led to friendship with you. At least to meet you.

Why did it take so long to find out? Why did that event take so long to jell? Why so little meaning then, and in three years time so crucial a turning point?

I didn't agree with those two men then — nor understand them — and I probably wouldn't entirely now. But that matter of opinions doesn't make much difference, does it? We don't have to have the same judgment about things, do we, so long as we have the same spirit? Their spirit I sensed. That made the difference. That was your Spirit, wasn't it?

Anyway, I can't agree exactly with the things they believed a generation ago. But I would like to believe with the same spirit — so long as it's yours.

So thank you for them and for their response to the leading of your Spirit. Thanks, also, for those other ten or twelve fellows. They must have been there in response to the same spirit. I've lost track of all of them. The only one I ever heard of again was Joe. Years later he wrote me a long, rambling, incoherent letter. I asked a friend to see him, and he said he'd had a breakdown and was put in a mental hospital. I haven't heard from him since, and I never wrote again.

But you haven't lost track of them, have you, Jesus?

You never lose track of anybody. You not only keep track of them, you keep trusting them — even when they let you down. You trusted those disciples, though they betrayed you. And, finally, they became trustworthy — but that was afterward, when you gave them your Spirit.

I'd like to be the kind of person who could introduce other people to you. So help me to trust that Spirit of yours that comes through people. There isn't any other way you can get to us, is there? There is no way you can get to anybody else except through us, is there? That means through me, doesn't it? So give me, I pray, that Spirit. Amen.

II

A LETTER TO A FATHER

Princeton, N.J.
April 12, 1936

Dear Dad:

The purpose of this letter is twofold: first, to answer your question about where I stand concerning education. Second, to let you know that I cannot accept the position you offer. I thank you very much. In many ways it would be fun working with you, but I have now decided to take the job in Turkey. Let me talk first philosophically and then personally.

Members of the teaching profession have an opportunity to contribute to society in two ways. One is to lead youth along the intellectual paths that they themselves have traveled; the other is to aid in the moral development of youth, in the building of their character. Preparation for the first is concrete and can be accomplished only by a high degree of intellectual development on the part of the teacher himself. The other quality is more subjective, but can be fostered by a study of the humanities, through touch with a vaster realm of thought.

While it is apparent that these two approaches can never be divorced completely one from the other, the college professor is more directly concerned with the intellectual growth of the student. As a general rule, contacts are maintained through the medium of the classroom, and the opportunities to exercise any influence, beyond arousing a sense of intellectual curiosity on the part of the student, are limited. While there are exceptions to this, generally the professor does not come into contact with the student outside the classroom, and there is little opportunity to influence the student through personal contact.

The situation in a secondary school is different. There the authority of the College Board Examinations determines what the line of intellectual development shall be. The teacher has no choice but to prepare the student for them, and any further intellectual exploration is usually out of the question. It is on this level, however, that the teacher has an opportunity, by personal contact, to make his influence felt on the moral growth of the student. This is especially important in his adolescent and formative years. Apart from the influence his religion will bring to bear, that teacher is best equipped who has been able to develop the broadest perspective, who has taken something himself from the great teachers of history.

Although the distinction here is somewhat artificial, I feel that the college professor's greatest contribution lies in opening new intellectual vistas for the student, and the secondary school teacher's is in helping the moral development of the student through a close personal relationship.

For one who has definitely decided upon the teaching profession, graduate work is, in certain cases, a necessity, and, in any case, a decided advantage.

Therefore, in the immediate future, I plan to gain two or three years' experience in teaching, then to undertake graduate work in history. It would then devolve upon me to pass the results of this experience on to the students with whom I come in contact, to help them live a more complete life. A combination of intellectual keenness and moral excellence — these are the qualities a true teacher must have.

You will already have observed how indebted I am to you. Maybe you'll say all I've done is steal your own ideas, which I suppose is true. In any case, the two poles of education that I refer to here — intellectual integrity and moral excellence —

are just about where I stand. They come, I know, from you —
though I can't say too much about your ability as a teacher
after that 37 I got in American history, thanks to your bright
tutoring.

What I don't refer to here is that other level of where religion fits into the picture. This is probably because I'm still
pretty fuzzy about what I do think. I don't have any question
about your own conviction that religion is meant to be involved all the way in life, and that's where the thing really
counts. If only we could adopt those ideas of yours that religion is supposed to be in everything that is beautiful and good
and all the rest of that in all aspects of life, then such questions as the virgin birth, immortality, and the more philosophical questions would no longer bother us quite so sharply.

I admit that this may not be exactly what your idea is, but
at least it's what I've gathered from you and from my own experiences and thoughts.

I can't accept for myself all those religious principles that
form part of the church which I know mean something to you.
As far as I'm concerned, the church itself might as well go
lose itself. All right, don't press me. That's probably too
strong. I can only say, I just don't get it. At least since I've
begun to form my own ideas on this subject, I don't get it;
though in the earlier years I will confess it meant something,
though I'm not sure just what — forgiveness, I guess, most of
all. The beautiful windows in the chapel here and the choir
may add a nice, religious atmosphere, but they seem to me to
strike some kind of superstitious or too emotional a note. If
the church can't get at us through our minds, it will do its
best to get at us through our emotions. Can't it somehow represent truth, reality, more clearly than it does?

I agree with you that we, of ourselves, haven't got enough
goods to keep us together as men, and the only thing that can
bind us in some form has to come from God, but whatever that
is, I think it is more inside us. I just don't get the connection

between that and the church. I'll be darned if I can explain
it, but it's a force that has continued, so that's why I suppose
I say prayers at night. It has to do with a power that's above
me and outside me and one with which I reflect before I go
to sleep at night. It tells me when I'm right, more or less. At
least there are certain things I do that I know I ought not to
do, and that comes to my help. It tells me that I ought to
write to Louise and tell her it's all over with us, but I still
don't obey it.

That reminds me — why don't you tell Louise? You're as
fond of her as I am.

Well, all of this is very involved and doesn't seem to make
much sense to me, but I know there's something there, if I can
only grasp it; and if I ever can grasp it, then I'll certainly be
a greatly improved person.

You'll be interested to know that a few weeks ago a preacher
here said, " Reason alone will not enable a man to withstand
successfully the temptations of evil." A man lives successfully,
he said, when he allows himself to be " transformed by surren-
dering to spirit instead of permitting himself to be regulated
solely by the intellectual force of reason." That's a quote from
a student paper. I think he's right, though I'm still not clear
about what spirit means. It can't be something just opposed
to, or apart from, reason or the flesh or anything else human,
can it? I should think that spirit was a part of all human life
and not some esoteric essence all by itself.

Sheer intellectualism isn't enough; right teachers aren't
enough, but if religion — and that I think is what he is talking
about when he refers to spirit — is to hold water, it's got to be
something more than just that. I could agree with it then, although I must say I don't think most of the guys around here
would, and you can hardly blame them. There has to be something more definite in this whole business, and whatever it is
certainly hasn't been explored deeply enough by me, nor have
I been exposed to it sufficiently, perhaps. So the thing sort of

plagues me, but I'm not in any position to do anything about it right now.

Now, let me be personal. I hope you will not be too disappointed by my decision and that you won't think that my going to take this other job means I'm repudiating your ideas, because I'm not. It's just that I've got to strike out on my own. There is nothing personal about it.

I get a little annoyed, I must confess, by the impression I get that you have the impression that I'm turning into an intellectual snob. I don't think that's the problem. I think the real problem in this kind of education is the danger of social self-satisfaction. We're the boys that have it made, and we don't have to take any interest in anybody else. It's a kind of complacency that's pretty easy to fall into.

I don't think I'm bright enough to be an intellectual snob — though I must say I've gotten a great deal out of the academic side these past two years, and there's just a hair's chance I'll make Phi Bete at the end of the year, but the real fun, of course, has been the enterprise itself. Mason and Reischauer have been tremendous. The former, particularly, has made me see what an idea is, and how it can shake you and flip you and toss you over on your ear.

So, if I'm going to go into teaching, I need to get some teaching experience, and it seems to me that it's just going to be a lot better for me to get that first experience a long ways away in another culture, where I might learn another language and come to know another part of the world. You know I'd like to spend a summer in Russia, anyway. So if I'm going to have to make a lot of beginning mistakes, I might as well make them five thousand miles away.

I'm sorry you got so exercised about my asking you for $200 last week. That's what I need to finish the college bills. I promise to pay back $150 by commencement time, when I'll get my final pay from the laundry job.

I'll be glad to stay around for two or three weeks in June

so that you can get away. I'm sorry you haven't been feeling all the best, and I'll be happy to do anything I can to be of help.

If you have any reflections about any of this, I'll be glad to have them. I guess I'd like to have your blessing on all this, but that may be asking too much.

My best love to Ma and the kids.

Love,

A Postscript

I hope, father, that you have forgiven me. I know you have. I knew you did long before you died. Oh, I know I disappointed you. You thought I was a bum at times. And so I was. But even when we disagreed about that job, I had a deep feeling that in the bottom of your heart you knew I had to be about our Father's business, and that meant saying no to you. And you were glad about it. Thanks for that good word of encouragement that came, even though you never said it. Thanks for that forgiveness.

It was only a little while ago that it came to me that I'd never forgiven you. The thought had never come to me before, but when it did, boy, did I ever forgive you.

Maybe I forgave you with so much enthusiasm because of what it did for me. It made *me* a new person. At least it made it possible for me to accept you and be a part of you as never before. So now I feel more whole, because I am more of a person. In a sense, I have become you. And still I am myself. Just more so.

I still don't know why you got so mad about that $200. But the hell with it. I'll find out someday.

Peace — brother — peace. And I mean *brother*.

Thanks, Jesus, for that Spirit of yours which brought each of us into our families, and in response to them made it possible to turn to thee. Thanks for all that brings us close to one another.

Thanks for making it possible for us to live forgiven. That's real freedom. And for helping our fathers (and everyone else) actually forgive us.

So let us live as new creatures right now. Amen.

III

A LETTER TO A COLLEGE FRIEND

Istanbul, Turkey
January 14, 1938

Dear Sam:

Many thanks for that good Christmas letter. I am delighted to know that things are even better in Africa than you had expected. You don't say very much about what you're doing, except that you're walking all the time. You don't say where you're walking, except it's in the back country. Where are you walking from? When you get to where you're going, what do you do then? Walk back again? I have real trouble picturing you in any monastery, but I suppose you can get used to anything. Next time you write, tell me what you do — both in the monastery and out.

Sorry to hear about your complaint. We have the same thing here, except we call it " Turkish Tummy." I had it last year for about two months. They finally put me in the infirmary and kept me on a diet of bananas and steak. There wasn't any improvement until I took the Orient Express to Ankara during the spring vacation. By that time I was so fed up I had two scotch and sodas on the train and haven't had a trace of the complaint since. Ask the monks if they can't provide you with that remedy.

That was a good trip we took last summer with Paul. It's not often that you can see two college friends, a sister of one,

Amalfi, Sorrento, a Polish princess, and a defrocked priest all
on the same trip. What a good evening we had with all of
them at your sister's, even if it did end with Paul falling down
the stairs and annoying your sister by making so much noise!
But it was really her fault for serving so much Chianti. I hope
he didn't break a leg, but I guess we'd have heard by this time
if he had.

I wonder why that priest was so keen on hearing about what
you were going to do and kept saying we both ought to go
into the ministry. That was certainly a long harangue he gave
us about the Holy Trinity. Remember when he got all through
and then asked, " Now, gentlemen, do you understand what
I've been saying? " And Paul said, " No, Father, I haven't understood a single damn word." Then he replied, " That's just
what I've been saying. It's a holy mystery."

That was as encouraging a word as I've heard about the
Christian faith in a long time. It's a great mystery. I guess it's
holy, but at least it's great.

There's not much news from this battlefront. Two things,
however, are going on. I'm not quite sure what they mean, either — perhaps they're a holy mystery, also.

The first is the girl I mentioned to you briefly last summer,
saying she'd just arrived here. She may turn out to be more
than simply a girl who's just arrived. We're seeing a fair
amount of each other, and it looks as though it might develop
into something. I'll know better after next summer when
we've been separated for a while. I know you'll make some
comment about having met a number of other girls I've known
and this may turn out to be the same case, but I somehow
don't think so.

The other thing has to do with this teaching. There were
two awful experiences last year that somehow related to each
other. I can't quite figure them out yet.

The first happened the first week in school when I was told
that I had to supervise study hall for eighty-five boys age 13 to
17. The task, of course, was to keep them quiet so they could

do their homework. That was tough when they didn't know any English and I didn't know any Turkish.

About two minutes after we had begun, they started humming. It went circling around the room. It was a baffling, almost terrifying experience. Everybody had his face in his book, apparently studying as hard as he could. There would be humming in one corner of the room, then it would subside and pop up in another, and then it would move around in circles. After a minute or so, I stood up and shouted, "Stop!" It stopped for a moment and then began again. I did that once more, and the same thing happened! More humming!

Then I don't know what got into me, but I jumped off the platform, went down, took hold of the first boy I could lay my hands on, cracked him across the side of the head as hard as I could, took him by the seat of the pants, threw him out of the room, said I never wanted to see him again, and slammed the door.

The humming stopped. I haven't had any trouble with discipline since then.

Later I discovered that this poor boy, whose name was Kemal Ardahanli, had been one of the real troublemakers in the school the previous year. His father, according to rumor anyway, was a brigand chief from Eastern Anatolia, who, for a number of years, had been an outlaw and only recently had received an amnesty from Attaturk. Kemal, apparently, felt he had to live up to his father's reputation and was continually in trouble. Perhaps it's just as well I cracked him rather than someone else. At least it established who was boss.

The other awful experience was a biology exam. When I gave the first six weeks' test, not only did everybody pass, but almost everybody got 90 or above. That was perfectly silly. I wasn't that good a teacher, and the Lord knows they weren't that good students. So the next day I gave them the same test all over again, but this time I stayed right in the room and watched them with a beady, eagle eye. Of course what happened was that this time about half the class flunked. It was

perfectly clear that on the first test, which had been an-
nounced, everybody had prepared by devising devious ways
of cheating — notes in shoes, under watches, in pockets, on ink
in the palm of their hands. You name it; they had it. The only
important thing was the mark they received.

This, it turns out, is part of the pattern of their lives. The
teacher is the enemy. You're meant to get away with just as
much as you can. The goal isn't knowledge; it's marks. The
teacher gives the marks, and you'd better get the best marks
you can in any way that you see fit. It's related in some fashion
to the authority structure, where the key figure is either the
father in the home, or the mayor in the village, or the teacher
in the school, or the imam in the mosque, or the chief of the
tribe, or the president of the republic. In one of the village
schools last year — just to show you how seriously they take
this — two teachers were shot by students for giving low marks.
It makes one a little uneasy.

Well, the point of this story is that this year that same class
is taking that same exam on the honor system. I suppose there
are two or three that cheat and get away with something, but
I'm sure that the vast majority now know that they have to
trust themselves, that honesty has some kind of meaning and
truth, and that you can't cheat and get away with it forever.
I've tried to teach them this scale of values — marks are least
important, knowledge is more important, honor is the most
important.

Now, there isn't any question that the success I've had is related to their personal relationship with me. That relationship
has been developed not simply in the classroom but, Lord
knows, I eat with these fellows, I put them to bed, I get them
up in the morning, play soccer, volleyball, basketball, go on
picnics with them. They've somehow come to trust me. The
fact is, I like the students very much. They know this. They
also know I'm the boss. After all, didn't I crack Kemal Ardahanli on the head?

There are a couple of things that aren't clear to me. At least in a place like this, you can't go around just being palsy-walsy to be a friend, putting your arms around him. That's perfectly silly. You're a teacher, not a buddy. There has to be some authority established. If there's no authority, then there's no respect.

Once there's authority established, then there's something to respect. Out of that respect, there has developed trust. That's the point where it's then possible for you to get over some ideas that you have, such as honesty is the best policy; or don't kick a boy when he's down; or don't cheat on examinations; or be a good sport when you lose a soccer game; or don't just walk off the field before the game is over because you are losing. If you're supposed to be quiet at night, for heaven's sake, be quiet. All these things are bound together.

Anyway, what seems to be evolving in my own head is the idea that there is something very basic and fundamental about things like honor and trust and sportsmanship and honesty. These are human values. They're pretty consistent human values, however, whether they're in Princeton, New Jersey, or in Istanbul, Turkey, or in Kalamazoo, Michigan. That's because they're human.

The question that's on my mind now is, Are these values anything more than human? If you grant that they belong to man, does that mean that they belong also to God — assuming there is a God? Do they, in fact, come from him?

That is the question. I've got to get moving on some answer to that by the time I leave here. Got any help for me there? Ask the monks. Maybe they can tell you.

Let's count on that meeting in Paris next summer if we possibly can. Maybe we can get Paul to join us for a week. How about your sister? We might even try the Polish princess and the defrocked priest.

I hope all continues to go well. When you write, tell me not only what you're doing but what monks do. Take care.

Love,

A Postscript

Well, Jesus of Nazareth, it takes us a long, long time to make any sense out of what you're doing with us, doesn't it? We begin by thinking that your only words to us are: " Thou shalt," " Thou shalt not," " Do this," " Don't do that."

We are wrong when we think of you as plaguing us with demands to be better men. " Stop watching that woman walk down the street — or on the beach. Stop that extra drink — or even the first one. Give that tithe before taxes, not after. Say your prayers all the time, not just on Sunday or once in a while. Give me your whole heart, not just part of it."

You aren't just a gadfly, irritating us with increasingly difficult requests so that we want to shoo you away, or hit back, or obey you to get rid of you — just, we hope, to keep you quiet.

But you don't stay quiet, do you? You always keep coming back to confront us. That's it. *You* confront us.

It's not really the demands that confront us. It is you. You are in the demands. You *are* the demands. We don't have to obey them; we have to obey you. It is you we are after, not your demands.

You are ours when we are poor in spirit and mourn and are meek; when we hunger and thirst after righteousness and are merciful, pure in heart, and peacemakers; when we are persecuted and reviled for your sake.

It is impossible — humanly impossible. And yet, of course, it is possible. It is your possibility — not ours.

It's not blasphemy, is it, to say that the spirit that bound Kemal and me is the same spirit that binds you and me? He and I became friends *through* the law. He broke it. He felt the clip on the ear. In time he knew I liked him. He trusted me. He took exams on the honor system. He wasn't obeying a law; he was responding to me. That spirit that bound us together (that was you, wasn't it?) became a part of him, and he lived in that spirit.

I hope he does now. Even though we don't know each other anymore, I hope he knows that spirit — knows you.

" Thy Kingdom come." That's not quite right, is it? It has come. You have come. Let us live as sons of the King — your sons — right where we are — in trust and in obedience. Then may the new life come.

May your law be written on our hearts. May *you* dwell there. Then the law and our hearts will be one and at peace. You and I will be at peace. Amen.

IV

A LOVE LETTER

Paris, France
July 14, 1939

Darling:

It looks like war, all right. The parade along the Champs
Élysées today was quite a different spectacle from the one
three years ago. At that time there were very few crowds on
the street. Those that were there were apathetic. There was a
listlessness about the city — except for the dancing in the
streets in the evening. The gendarmes were in their busses on
every side street off the Champs Élysées ready to quell any
riots that might flare up around the issue of the civil war in
Spain. All the energy then seemed to be directed toward
checking the dangers of the civil conflict and keeping the con-
servative and radical forces under control.

Today that was all changed. The line of parade from Place
de la Concorde to L'Étoile was just jammed — everybody
seemed to be out. The rumbling of the tanks, one after the
other, and the roaring of the planes in formation after formation made quite a noisy morning.

Beyond any question, the general feeling is that war is going to break out. It's simply a matter of how soon. The American Express, of course, is jammed with people, hectic in their
desire to get back, but it's something you sense in the atmosphere more than any concrete information.

All of which means, I think, that you and your mother and sister had better make definite plans immediately to go to the States. Since your father's death, there seems to be no reason why you should stay on.

Besides which, I'd feel a good deal happier with you on the other side of the Atlantic. I know this is selfish. I know it's tied up with my just naturally wanting to see you and be with you. In my best moments I'd like to think also that it really is the soundest counsel you can get. Will you please talk it over?

I'll see what can be done about a job for you in New York when I get back, but probably there won't be anything I can do other than line up a few opportunities, because the people will want to see you. But once they see you, they'll hire you! No doubt about that.

I leave the first thing tomorrow morning for Le Havre, and since it will be six days before I can mail the next letter, let me bring you up to date.

It's been wonderful to be back in this city. Even with the war just around the corner, there is something about the beauty of this place — its romance, I guess, is the word — that once it takes possession of you, it never leaves you. You remember Mac saying that when he came back to Paris the first time after twenty-five years he just stood on the street corner and cried. It certainly is the city of poets, artists, writers, and lovers. All kinds of people have written about their love for it. It's really quite a miracle that the gas fumes from the busses should smell like perfume. It's strange, because it's so universal an experience, and yet it's so personal for everybody, a kind of fey spirit of romanticism about it. It's almost as though this were the way life really ought to be. Too bad it isn't. Yet, somehow, that spirit possesses the city.

The Orient Express got in on schedule yesterday — that is, about twelve hours late. There was plenty of time in the evening, however, for me to walk once again across the Pont Neuf and then up the Rue Dauphine. The latter will remain in my mind forever because that's where I first met bedbugs

three years ago. When I went to the doctor about the swell-
ings and itchings, he took one sharp look and then laughed.
" This is a painful, but not fatal, disease," he said. " Now, let
me introduce you to some of the facts of life that you probably
were never taught in the States." His first prescription:
" Change hotels."

Even more vivid than that is the memory of the first night
in Paris, sitting in one of those little alcoves of stone benches
on the Pont Neuf beside the statue of Henri IV, looking west-
ward as the sun was setting, and being absolutely overwhelmed by the immensity of utter, unexpected, unanticipated
joy. I was free of every single tie in the world. I didn't have to
do a thing, was accountable to nobody, could sleep as late,
stay up as late, walk as late, read as late — do anything I
wanted to under the sun.

Most of this was really just the simple sense of freedom at
getting away from the family. Still, there was something even
deeper than that, an exhilaration of the spirit such as I'd never
known. It was almost as though I could put out my hand
and embrace the whole world — or at least the city of Paris
— and eat, drink, sleep, and love all human existence. That
was a red-letter day — or a red-letter evening. Then I got
up and walked back toward Notre Dame, stopped in a bistro,
and ordered a " sandwich jambon." It turned out to be a ham
sandwich. That was a great surprise, and very satisfying.

So last night as I sat there and thought about that freedom
from ties, I thought, isn't this interesting, now? Three years
later I have new ties. These are the ties with you, and I thank
the Lord for them.

The sense of exhilaration and freedom I have now is a little
bit different, although, somehow, it's related to what I experienced three years ago as I sat on the same bench. The kind
of freedom that I have in my relationship to you isn't simply
to be myself and do what I want to; it's somehow freedom to
trust myself in a way I never have before. Sounds a little

corny, but I think it means I'm now free really to commit myself in love as I never have before.

Both of these evenings were exhilarating, but in different
ways. I suppose now what I'm saying is that you're really meant
to be able to love yourself and to trust yourself, but you
can't really do that until you are rid of all the ties that burden
you and keep you from being yourself (or at least ones that
you think keep you from being yourself, which is almost the
same thing). Once you are free of those ties, then it's possible
to love another human being and to commit yourself.

Or the fact is, it may be just the other way around. It's
only when you are loved by somebody else that you can ever
love yourself and, then, finally be yourself. Maybe that's more
like it. That's why this type of freedom is in a deeper sense
not just trying to get your own way, but it is in discovering
that the only way you can really get your best way is in a
relationship to somebody else.

When I was here before, I read a book by Léon Blum, the
socialist, who also apparently prided himself on knowing the
ways of women. Anyway, he wrote a book in which he said
that he was able to look at a woman and tell whether she had
ever been loved or not. I don't know how absolutely true this is,
but there isn't any question but that there is some kind of
confidence that is expressed by a woman who knows that she
is loved and admired. She walks in a certain kind of way; she
has control of herself, confidence in herself, self-respect. I guess
that's what it is. You can affirm yourself, not try to protect
yourself, if someone says you're worth affirming.

A nice negative illustration passed me this morning on the
street — a fat and dumpy woman about thirty walked by
smoking a cigarette, all slouched over with a hangdog expression. She looked puffy and unhealthy. Certainly, she didn't
look as though anybody had ever loved her for even two
and a half seconds. Well, I love you anyway. That's one thing
I know. So walk straight, chest out, tummy in. No need for me

to say this, of course, because you always have. I guess that's
because people always loved you. I don't blame them.

This means that a person becomes a whole person, fully
himself as a person, only when he's loved. If he's not loved,
he somehow gets ground down.

Maybe the whole dating process through school and college and afterward is to try to test people out; and as you
test them, you test yourself, both to see whether you can
trust them and whether you can trust yourself. Then, if
there's somebody you can trust, there's a chance you can
love that person. Or is it the other way around? Love makes
it possible to trust someone. No, that's not it, because people
love people they don't trust sometimes. I guess maybe it's
both, because you don't love everybody you trust, either. It's
all mixed together. Love is stronger than trust even; love is
more important than trust. Well, when there can be both trust
and love, then I guess there can be marriage. Without it,
there's not going to be a whole marriage, which is just
simply another way of saying I love you and I trust you.

Anyway, what was on my mind when I started this was
to say that this drive to love, to find wholeness in relationship to another person, is just part and parcel of the human
enterprise. Biologically, it is expressed through sex, but it's
always a great deal more than simple physiological activity.
All sex drive is directed toward another person. That's what
brings completion or fulfillment or wholeness. It's not sex
mechanics, though that's involved, but it's sex spirituality,
if I can use that word, that is the whole person. Sexuality
is spirituality, or it can be spirituality. No, it *is* spirituality.
Is that right? Well, spirituality includes sexuality. That's the
better way to put it. Or is it the other way around — sexuality
includes spirituality? No, that can't be the whole truth, though
it's true enough. Which is more powerful: sex or spirit? Maybe
that can't be answered because they are both so completely
intertwined. That's another curious mixture, like love and
trust. At least the negative is true — there is no such thing as

sex apart from spirit, or spirit apart from sex. Not for man, there isn't.

I'm just trying to say I miss you, and I don't feel whole without you.

Yet, in a curious way, I must confess (I hope you won't be offended by this) that there is even good about being apart. Somehow, you can know even more about yourself (and, perhaps, the other self as well) when the physical presence is removed. Sex sometimes gets in the way. I don't know if this would be true if we knew we were to be separated from each other forever, but when we know the separation is going to be overcome in another month or year, then maybe insights come on a deeper level than they do by simply being together all the time.

What brought all this up was my memory of a trip to Chartres that first summer here. I was staying at the same hotel on Rue St. André des Arts where a fellow I used to go to camp with years ago was staying. He was traveling that summer with a very nice girl. They were not only traveling together, they were living together, and marriage, apparently, wasn't in their prospects at all. I saw a fair amount of them for about ten days, and one day we took a trip down to Chartres. That was a great experience, not simply because of that magnificent cathedral, but because of some kind of insight that has come to me since then. I remember sitting in a third-class compartment. They were right across from me, holding hands. We were laughing and talking and having just a very good time. In a little string bag that French women have she had brought a loaf of bread and some cheese and a bottle of wine. After we'd had luncheon, they sat back and put their arms through each other's. I thought, that's what life is really about when you've got two people together who can love, be happy, kiss each other, hold each other, laugh and kid with each other. I looked at her and her eyes sparkled, and she was just plain beautiful. I thought, that's what life is meant to be.

After we walked around the cathedral together for a while, they went off. I stayed inside and sat down near the crossing on the left-hand side, just sitting and looking at the high altar. The light was coming in through the west window. It was toward the end of the afternoon. I turned around and looked at the light streaming through the magnificent colors for a while. Then I sat around again and looked upward and tried to take in the vastness of all that was represented there. I hadn't read Henry Adams' book at that time, but ignorant as I was, I thought, if ever there was a cathedral that was a cathedral, this is it.

Then, somewhat to my surprise, as I hadn't seen her come in, I noticed, a few pews in front of me and slightly to the side, a young widow dressed in black. She was, I suppose, about twenty-five years old. She was kneeling, praying. Suddenly I was overwhelmed by this feeling of infinite compassion for her. What a terrible thing, I thought, for a person as young as this to lose her husband. And now, of course, she has to come in and pray to God, because this is the only place she can get any solace or consolation.

But as I watched her, I saw that, while she obviously was praying, she wasn't seeking consolation. She was a part of something going on that was different from that. I'm not sure what it was, but she wasn't asking for anything or feeling sorry for herself. Actually, there was a beauty about her face that came from the inside. Her features weren't particularly attractive, but there was a radiance or, if you'll pardon the phrase, a glow that came out of her. Even more than that, there was a strength that came through.

I thought, that's a strange thing. Here I've been thinking of my friend's girl, how wonderful she looked, and how beautiful, and how, somehow, that kind of love she and he had for each other was what made the world go round. Now, two hours later, here's another young girl, more or less the same age, who obviously has loved and been loved, and now that's broken, and yet the beauty this girl has is deeper than the

other girl's. There was just something deeply satisfying in
the beauty and the strength that came out of that young
woman. It was about as close to a religious experience as I
ever had.

She was obviously in touch with something deeper than her
husband's hands. She couldn't hold those hands any longer,
and yet there was no question about her fulfillment and completion. She was a whole person if I ever saw one. Could it be
that she was in touch with something else beyond her?

She certainly was convinced that she was and that that
relationship was more real to her than any other relationship.
Actually, maybe it was more real than her relationship to her
husband. Perhaps it was her relationship with her husband
that made this one possible.

Well, I just want to say that in something of the same kind
of sense you are more real to me now than you are at certain
times even when we are together. How do you account for
that? Can it be that, because we are separated, it's now possible for my spirit to be in touch with your spirit on a deeper
level than when we're together? I suppose that if love is
eternal, the answer is, yes, it is possible.

This just makes me miss you all the more. I'm not sure that
this is the way I'd feel if I knew you were never going to
come back to the States, or if I were never going to see you
again, or if you or I died, or something like that. As it is,
I have a nice deep feeling that I'm pledged, that, therefore,
everything is going to be all right, because somehow I'm
pledged in love. I think maybe that's what that girl in Chartres had: she was pledged in love — her husband's love — but
something more, too.

I'll hope to get some letters when I get home because
they'll help bridge the ocean. This separation is bearable
when all is said and done because I know that in time, sometime, you'll bridge that ocean too, and we'll be together again.
That will be a great reunion.

Perhaps that's what all this means, that love is not just union.

It's the union and reunion, or union, separation, and coming together again. Maybe that's what makes the world go round after all, not just knowing yourself once and knowing another, but knowing that the coming and the going in love is part of a deeper love that comes. They are all mixed together, somehow.

Anyway, best to the rock pile and love to all.

My deepest love to you,

A Postscript

So, Jesus of Nazareth, it was no accident that when you came to bear witness to yourself, the first people you let in on the secret were those gathered for a wedding.

That was a good place to do it, for a wedding always speaks to everybody there. The love received and pledged there by a man and a woman in a company of people reminds everybody in that company who they are — that they are lovers, too. They get reminded just once more that they are members of one another because they are members of Christ and he is the one who keeps turning the human into the divine.

When you turned the water into wine at Cana, you made it clear that the elemental things of life — food and drink and sexuality — are bearers of divine possibilities. The more human, the more divine — nothing is not divine when it bears love.

So help us to see you and respond to you in all these ways that you communicate with us. Behind and through and in our beloved, may we know it is you with whom we have dealings. So may we, who are in love, love each other the more. And in that love, love you.

May we rejoice in it as we hope one day to be worthy of it.

Let us rejoice in our life in your body, our life with your members. Let us forbear with one another in love. Let us be patient with differences, quiet when we are exasperated, content to bear a little cross for our common life, that together we may live by the power of your holy cross.

Bless, we beseech you, your church and every member of the same, as we each bless in you and for you those members who are bearers of your love to us. Amen.

V

A LETTER TO A BISHOP

New York City
May 18, 1942

Dear Bishop:

Thank you very much for your letter indicating your willingness to take me on as a candidate for the ministry. I shall try to answer your questions about the reasons that have caused me to come to this decision.

Perhaps the first thing to be said is the negative word that I never had any long-term idea of going into the ministry. There has been no planning for it — at least, not consciously — there has been no philosophy, Christian or otherwise, behind it. This decision is not the end result of a "projected plan for my life."

You might say it just sort of happened. Each step that I have taken has seemed at the time to have been the right step. I am now about to graduate from seminary, and I think the next logical step is for me to go into the ministry.

The positive factors sort themselves out in my mind in the following way.

First, in the background, of course, is my family, and particularly my father — you will recall that both my father and mother worked in the East Side of New York under the auspices of the church in what we would call today "social work." For the last twenty years of his life, my father had been a Christian clergyman in education.

The more immediate foreground since college has been occupied with teaching. Human values had a large part in this, but the church has had (apart from two or three personal experiences) no place at all. It is not simply that the official work of the church was forbidden in the country where I served, but it was just not a significant factor in my own thinking.

There is something fascinating about teaching, the passing on of some knowledge that you already possess in such a way that it begins to become part of the personality of another human being. Of course there were a lot of failures — probably more failures than successes — but the satisfactions of seeing a young mind take hold of an idea that you have given to him, respond to it, make it part of himself are, I think, greater than any other human satisfactions. In my own experience this was partially intellectual knowledge, but it was also knowledge concerned with behavior or values — such concepts as honor, integrity, sportsmanship, honesty. These are, to be sure, very simple human virtues in American education (although probably never observed as fully as we like to think they are), but these are not natural assumptions in other cultures. The persistent question that plagued me during those years was, Is there anything universally valid about these ideas or concepts?

Philosophically, I was asking the question that Plato answered with his Ideas but was given an unusual opportunity to try to wrestle with them personally. My own conviction gradually came to be that at least there was something in the experience of human beings which pointed to a common thread where such values as trust, commitment, concern for another, honesty, helping one another did strike a common human chord. They rang true to human experience — anyway, at least to my limited experience.

This led me, then, to the next obvious question: Was there any way in which I could pursue on a wider scale the search to see if these human values were represented in any transcendent values? This interest was an infinitely more pressing one for me personally than simply an intellectual one. This meant that I was not as interested in the sheer academic or intellectual life as I was in the relationship between that world of truth and the living experiences of men. At that time, I think I was reasonably well committed in my own mind to a future of teaching, but I felt that a period of preparation in an atmosphere where I could deal with this deeper problem would be helpful.

The only logical place seemed to be seminary. It is interesting to observe that on the American educational scene there appears to be no other place to go if you are interested in wrestling with the personal meaning of ideas. When I went, there was no idea — again, at least not in my conscious mind — that I would go into the ministry. I hadn't been to church more than a dozen times in three years.

I had in a vague way been aware of a " something other " in my life. It would have been impossible to have defined it. I didn't really pray to " it." I was simply conscious that I was not alone. On two or three occasions there was a sense of its " breaking in " on my thoughts — once very sharply. This, of course, may have been my unconscious that "welled up" rather than "broke in." The distinction seems unimportant. What does seem important is the recognition that something was going on within me and around me which was in some relation to me and which was something other than my own self.

The first three years at seminary have, I think, done two things:

First, they have opened the doors to the vast and exciting world of Christian thought. There certainly is no limit to the intellectual challenge that exists within the Christian faith. I had no idea that the " truths " of Christianity were such tremendously shattering concepts that have to do with the whole of ultimate reality and the relationship of that reality to man. In a very naïve fashion, I had just assumed that the Christian faith was concerned with loving God and man. That is true on one level, but exactly what that means intellectually is a challenge that demands all the mind and integrity that a man possesses.

The most exciting intellectual experience was a seminar on Calvin and Luther conducted by Tillich. I had had a course with him junior year in Greek philosophy, which went right over my head. I hardly caught a phrase that he gave in his lectures, much less any idea that he was trying to convey. This last year, however, I finally was able to catch on. Each week one member of the seminar would prepare a paper on one aspect of the thought of Luther or Calvin and then present his own point of view. Tillich, each time, would then take the man's own point of view and, on the basis of those presuppositions, would lead a class discussion down the path, step by step, to see what the final conclusions of that position would be in relationship, not only to Luther or Calvin, but to the whole world of Christian thought — indeed, of secular thought as well. He always supported you in your position, and by the time he'd finished taking you where he said your thoughts led, you were quite encouraged about your own ability. As a result, he helped most of us feel that we were very professional thinkers indeed. At least we had been in touch with a great mind, and our own minds were stretched to the uttermost. We probably got more of Tillich than either Luther or Calvin, but since it is the twentieth century we are living in, that is, no doubt, all to the good.

The other lesson the seminary has taught me is that the Christian faith is concerned with society just as much as with individual people. I had been interested in social movements and political organization, but it had never occurred to me to take seriously the Christian claim that it was meant to be a creative social force. I had thought generally of the church bringing the dead hand of the past to oppose social change. Religion has always been a social force, either for ill or for good, as it has always been embedded in society.

Christian faith, therefore, is as much concerned about the relationship of nations and the relationship of social forces within nations as it is with the relationship in families. There is a law in the very structure of life itself, that is, the law of love. Violate it and you get broken; obey it and you live. That's the law of life. It's just as true in the relationship of corporate enterprises to corporate enterprises as it is in personal life; and just as true in the family of nations.

As a result of this, my very naïve pacifism got knocked right on the head and thrown out the window. I have respect for those Christian idealists who abide by a Christian pacifist position, but I think they are unable to bear witness except in a very personal way and certainly in no way that is effective, given the power structure of societies and how societies have to wrestle with power. Justice between power groups in society is just as much a concern of the Christian faith as love between persons. The church has a responsibility to make this clear.

The point I want to make, however, is not particularly one about pacifism, although, obviously, this is the issue in these days — there will be other issues in other days — but, rather, the social dimension of the Christian faith. The key figure, of course, is that great prophet, Reinhold Niebuhr.

Finally, I cannot recount what seminary has meant to me without saying just a word about the men whom I've come to know here who themselves are going into the ministry. They have been a powerful influence. It is through them that the ideas of the Christian faith have become personalized.

There has been a very fine group of friends who are perfectly normal human beings, who are concerned that their lives count for something, and who feel that the Christian faith has the most to offer contemporary society and are willing to identify themselves with it. I think it is in those long night sessions with three or four friends, when you break the great concepts into little bites that you can chew on yourself and, therefore,

digest some of the truth of the Christian faith, where the
real work of Christian conversion takes place.

The specific issue that has brought the ministry to the fore
now is the war. After volunteering for the Army and being
turned down because of a bad elbow, I was assured that this
physical disability would be waived if I were applying for
the chaplaincy. Given my convictions about what is important in life and what the Christian faith has to say about life,
this seems to me to be a very natural step for me to take now.
What I'll do after the war I have no idea, but I have no
reservations in my own mind about my desire to commit myself to the enterprise in which this nation has embarked, to
be identified with the men who are part of it, and in some
way to represent a truth that transcends all the division and
bitterness of war and that holds some promise for a more just
social order after the war — that is, the church.

My father, incidentally, thinks I am wrong. He says he's
known only about four Christian clergymen in his life and
one Christian bishop, and if I go around preaching, the
danger is I myself will become a castaway. He may be right,
but I think I will take the risk.

Thank you again for your kindness to me. Please let me
know if there is any further information you would like to
have.

Sincerely yours,

A Postscript

Why, Jesus of Nazareth, do you ask us to take no thought
for the morrow? We can't do that. We are men.

Animals don't live from day to day. Squirrels don't. They
store up their hoard of nuts for the winter. Why ask us to do
something you don't even ask of squirrels? Are not we of
much more value than they?

You seem to be asking us not to be men anymore. Part of
what it is to be a man and part of his greatness is that he can

plan for the future. He can lift himself up above himself and peer ahead and see what the lay of the land is and how he can best deal with it. When you ask us not to do this, you are asking us to renounce our manhood.

Yet you came to set us free so that we might live as sons of God. That means to be set free from our own plans and hopes for the future — not to be enslaved by them or by fear of losing them. It is to sit loose to them. Not to put our trust in them. Not to commit ourselves to any plan.

But to commit ourselves to you. Then — if we take our work where we are, to do the best work we can for you now — the future will take care of itself. To be responsible for our present work we plan for its future — but our trust is in you. Is that what you mean, Jesus of Nazareth?

Not to work less, but to work more. Not to be less human, but more human; not less worldly, but more.

But our trust is in none of these things. Our trust is in you.

Thanks, then, for not letting me see what I was getting in for when I first went to seminary. I would have died if I'd thought it meant the ministry. And now I know I'd be dead if it hadn't.

Thanks for keeping the future hidden and asking us only to trust you in the present. Then you can reveal yourself to us step by step.

So help us simply to trust you step by step. Grant that the way to holiness for us now may be in the work you have given us to do now. May it be in self-surrender to you. Then our future is all yours. Amen.

VI

A LETTER TO A WIFE

Tientsin, China
Decemeber 3, 1945

Darling:

The scuttlebutt is that in the next day or so we are going to get orders to return to Japan, pick up troops, and then head for the West Coast. From there the ship will proceed to be decommissioned some place or other. Of course, I don't know whether there's any truth to this or not, but it's all a reasonably intelligent guess. There may be a chance that we'll be back by Christmas, or at least by the first of the year. You can count on my giving you a ring the moment we land.

Anyway, there's no question but what things are winding up so far as this ship is concerned. The end is in sight. This letter will give me a chance to try to put down any summing up I can make about the last year and a half out here.

First of all, let me say that we have just gotten back from a thirty-six-hour liberty in Tientsin. We are now anchored off Taku Bar. I went up the river with Bert, and we stayed at the home of some White Russians who are in business, running what we would call a department store. They say they hope that the Communists will take over. That was a shocker. In their judgment it is clear that the Nationalists are unable to establish order and that they are so shot full of corruption that they never will be able to bring stability. They say that at least the Communists are honest; you know exactly where you stand with them. That's some commentary by a family who, twenty-five years ago, fled from the Communists in Russia and now are willing to embrace the Communists in China — all for the sake of a little principle like honesty. It shows how bad things are.

We brought about fifteen hundred Marines from Okinawa. Interestingly enough, the trip up here was the first trip where there was any violent dislike for the assignment given us. There has been the normal amount of griping aboard over the assignments that have come our way, but always within the framework of the knowledge, or conviction anyway, that we knew what our ultimate task was, which was to defeat the enemy, and we knew who the enemy were.

Since V-J Day, though, it seems as though suddenly we all have sprouted our political wings and are going to keep flapping them. There is hardly anybody on this ship that thinks that it is a wise thing for the United States government to be doing — this sending in of Marines to keep order. How on earth can the United States establish order throughout a country the size of China — particularly when the people of China (like our White Russian friends) are eager for any change and are willing to trust the Communists?

It's surprising, as a matter of fact, how little political talk there has been up to now. There has been almost no discussion for the past eighteen months about matters of national policy. Even the establishment of the United Nations didn't spark much discussion. It was as though we had individually committed ourselves to a cause, and we would try to carry out our part of it as well as we could, but we weren't going to get unduly exercised about the long-term policy or strategy. Maybe that's a kind of ostrichlike way to behave, but I think that's the fact of the matter.

About the only exception to that was the night in Zamboanga, when we heard the announcement of the bombing of Hiroshima. That seemed to us to be a real clincher, to promise

that the war would come to an end sooner than otherwise.
There was just a general sense of deep satisfaction that the
United States had the atomic bomb rather than the Japanese;
and that perhaps we wouldn't have to go through that invasion after all. The whole question that is being raised
in some of these church periodicals that have now reached
us about the moral issue seems to me to miss the point
entirely — either that, or I'm morally obtuse myself. Nobody
here, however, has the slightest question about the morality
involved. If you're committed to a war that is a moral mess
anyway, it's hard to draw the line as to where you stop before
driving as hard ahead as you can to stop the whole thing.
Anyway, for what it's worth, I think Mr. Truman was dead
right, and I'm not impressed by the sensitive consciences of
church officials who sit in offices in New York City.

So much for the international front. As you can see, those
big political issues don't occupy much of our time. Generally,
it's the more personal things, or very personal, like, what's
the best whorehouse in Tientsin? It didn't take very long for
a good number of the men on this ship to get a little experience so they could discuss this question. It's really kind
of funny taking one of these small boats up the river and
passing the time of day with the men; and then once we've
landed — zoom, off they go.

The impression I think I'm going to take home of these
men — the overwhelming impression — is of their goodness.
It's a strange thing to say, when it's perfectly obvious that
their moral behavior leaves a good deal to be desired and when
you realize that, because they have a nature common to all
men, they really are selfish and corrupt.

Yet there is, somehow, a deep note of goodness in these
guys that strengthens you and makes you a better person
yourself just because you have been with them. I'm not talking about their sexual behavior or their drinking. As a matter
of fact, remember that drinking in Manila which I told you
was so awful that the men had to be lifted aboard by cargo

nets — well, it turned out to have been due as much to poison
as to heavy drinking. The bottles labeled " Johnny Walker
Scotch " were filled with some kind of pineapple poison, and
somebody made a lot of money.

Anyway, the goodness of these men goes a good deal
deeper than the superficial, fleshly level. Maybe the word
" goodness " is wrong. I guess it's trustfulness I'm talking
about. That is, they trust each other, they rely on each other,
they care about each other. That old phrase, " He's my buddy,"
sounds as corny as can be, but it's just exactly the right word
for these men to use — a real buddy system that goes through
the whole ship.

A part of this, of course, is that when you're on a ship,
you have to learn to trust each other. Your life depends on it.
If you're a gunnery officer, you have to trust that the men
know what they're doing, and they have to trust you that
you know what you're telling them to do. When you're unload-
ing small boats in the pitch dark, you have to learn to trust
everybody to do their job as they're supposed to, because,
Lord knows, you can't straighten them out then. It's too late
when the boats are halfway over the side.

But it's something deeper than that even. It's a kind of
esprit de corps that gets developed when you're together
doing a common job and knowing that you belong to each
other. A perfect example is one of the warrant officers who
was a chief bo'sun's mate before the war and had spent
twenty years in China. Well, you just imagine what this
fellow looks like; and no matter how wild or typical you think
you've got it figured out, he's just a little bit more. He's over-
weight, his stomach hangs over his trousers, he smokes a big
cigar, he rolls when he walks. He can't open his mouth without a whole series of oaths following one another, and he's
just about the best Christian guy I've ever met in my life.
He'll do anything for anybody on this ship.

He loans the men money when they go on liberty — no
questions asked. He stands near the quarter deck, and any-

body that comes up and asks him for money, he gives it to them.

I asked him about this once. He said that when he was a seaman second class, he was in a jam, and a chief on that ship loaned him $25 and said, " I'll do it on one condition. Whenever you find that you've got a buddy in trouble, you'll help him out, too."

He said, "I've never forgotten that. I suppose over the years I've loaned well over $25,000 to shipmates just like this. I don't keep track of repayment, but my guess is that there's not more than one or two fellows that haven't repaid me, and that's probably because they got transferred while they were away." That's some record of Christian steward-ship, if you ask me.

Of course, some of the loyalties are limited. The concept of honesty, for example, is a very important one: "Don't cheat a buddy." When I got on this ship, coming out from San Francisco, the wardroom gossip was that this warrant officer was going to get the exec because he was convinced that on the last trip the exec had been cheating at bridge.

Before we got to Eniwetok, the executive officer stopped playing bridge. The warrant officer had just creamed him by cheating him back at his own game and taken $5,000. The exec said that closed out his bank account, and he had to stop. Served him right!

That's one of the principles. You don't cheat a shipmate; you've got to be honest with him.

Troops, on the other hand, are the enemy. You don't have to have any moral scruples about cheating troops when you carry them. I've watched sailors shoot craps in the galley and shift the dice between loaded and unloaded ones, depending upon whether army troops were playing or not. If any soldiers got into the game, then the loaded dice went to work. When they left, then a good clean honest game of craps started again.

Well, that's not a very elevated reflection, I suppose, but

it's the one I'm going to carry with me until I die — that men, by and large, just have a natural goodness about them. I suppose that that's bad Christian theology and that the heart of man is naturally corrupt; yet that's not the whole story by a long shot. There is something just naturally good about men, too.

It's something like natural religion, I guess. It would be silly to say that there's no such thing as natural religion. All you have to do is see what happens to some men in the face of nature and watch their religious response. Most nights after supper I try to get a little exercise by walking on the signal bridge. There are three or four of us who do it. It not only gives us some exercise and fresh air, but it gives us a chance to look at the sunset.

The signal officer is usually up there. He commented once: " Well, Chaplain, I'm really pretty much of a bum so far as my religion is concerned (he comes from a Jewish background), but I must say it does something to me to see the sun go down and these violent colors come out and shift around and linger and then they, too, finally are covered by darkness. I know it's not God, but it sure does remind me of God. I'm not sure it makes me a better guy, but it humbles me; so, if I've got any religion left at all, I guess that's about it."

If that's about it, and that is about it for lots of fellows, so be it. It certainly isn't the fullness of any Christian revelation, but it's something, and I have to confess it even means something to me, too. There was a time when I thought that this was just sentimentalism, and I repudiated sunsets; but after this time out here, sunsets are back in good standing.

Strangely enough, the goodness of men and the beauty of nature are, I think, impressions that are going to be more lasting than the church services. The only exception, of course, was that dramatic service of Holy Communion on V-J Day in Tokyo Harbor. That was moving beyond description.

We were sailing abeam of the *Missouri* while the peace

treaty was being signed. You could hear the radio on the fan-tail describing this. The convoy covered the whole harbor as far as your eyes could carry, and waves of planes went back and forth over the convoy. The service was topside because it was such a good day, and I suppose well over half the people received Communion, nearly a thousand men. It was just row after row after row of guys with their hands out, holding them up to receive something. That was the miraculous thing about it for me. They wanted to receive something; that's why they were there. So they just held their hands up.

They apparently couldn't define any doctrine of the Real Presence in the Sacrament. That wasn't important. What was important was that they knew that they were dependent on somebody other than themselves. They didn't know what on earth was going to happen once they landed, and here, in the breaking of the bread in this service, there was symbolized something that somehow struck deep into their hearts — into the hearts of all of us. That was a great service.

Other than that, the services followed pretty much of a pattern. As we approached the landing stages for each invasion, the services became better and better attended, and after the invasion was completed and we started going away, they became less and less well attended. This, some people would say, was another illustration of foxhole religion and didn't mean anything.

I am not at all sure about that. Foxhole religion describes one very natural part of human existence — when you're in trouble, you need help. I don't see anything the matter with that — at least it's a bridge into an understanding of the Christian faith. Besides which, there certainly isn't any point in condemning men for turning to God because they are men.

Well, that's about it, I guess. Everything continues in a pretty routine manner. I get in an hour of work on the Bible each day and an hour's reading. I hope I can keep that up when I get back. I also get in some chess in the evening. So far, I've won two games out of fifty.

It's a strange thing, but now that it's pretty clear that the end is going to come, and sooner rather than later, things begin to fall into perspective. There were times when the only prayer I was ever able to offer at the end of the day was, "Thank God I got through that day." Then gradually it became, "God, thank you for getting me through another day." Lately it's, "Thanks for the day." It's really best when I can just say, "Thanks."

I thank him for you too, toots. One kiss for Tom; two thousand for you.

All best love,

A Postcript

Jesus, I am thinking of those men in South Vietnam now.

Some of them are undoubtedly fighting with deep conviction about the rightness of their cause.

Lots of them are probably very uneasy about what they are doing.

Most probably haven't the vaguest idea, have no deep conviction. They're just there. Their number came up.

So, I hope they will have some idea of you, anyway, some sense of your presence. How can they get that? Maybe as they belong to a good outfit, with a good second lieutenant. Maybe as each really has a buddy. Maybe even a bar girl can comfort him, or a letter from home. Anyway, I hope you can. You keep them in mind, won't you?

Of course you do. That's what you were about two thousand years ago. Making that clear to us. Thanks. I'll thank you for them, too.

The best thanks I can give is by taking my life as it comes, and when I respond to it, try to respond to you and trust you rather than myself. Thanks for that, too. Don't let me shy away from my responsibility to my fellowmen. Help me to be intelligent and concerned about the country and what is happening to it. Make me, force me, to take my share in making it conform more to your will.

If a girl screams for help on a dark night, don't let me run for cover, but go help her. If I can't solve the racial crisis in the country, at least I can open doors in the building where I work and find jobs — and so open hearts. If the disadvantaged don't get help from the advantaged, to whom do they turn? Don't let me be a party to driving them to the wall. Keep me from walking around on the other side.

Since we've all been created equal, let us trust each other as equals — better, as brothers. Don't ever let me think that our nation gives that equality. God gives it. Help me help our country show forth that quality by justice for all. Let me give Caesar all my deepest social concern, my energy, and my intelligence, and to God, my heart and my trust.

What did you say, Jesus?

Oh, you said, " As you did it to one of the least of these my brethren, you did it to me." (Matt. 25:40.)

I see. Amen.

VII

A LETTER TO A TEACHER

Amherst, Mass.
June 9, 1953

Dear Bob:

Many thanks for your letter. I'm glad to know your new
assignment is going well. We miss you in the Connecticut
Valley, but are sure that your work in trying to communicate
what the ministry is all about to the next generation is even
more important than your work here with the girls. Maybe
not as much fun, but that's life.

I am honored that you would ask me to try to put into
writing how I would now define my ministry. That is very
sneaky of you. If you get letters like this from a dozen of
your old friends, then you will have your lectures all written
for a semester. Very typical of you! I'm only kidding, of
course.

Your question is too fancy. I can't answer it. It is too propo-
sitional and implies that I have a theological framework within
which I carry out my ministry. I did once. I don't now. All
I have now is one thing — a sense of a personal relationship
with God. It's not a very strong one, and it wavers all over
the place, but once in a while everything else falls away and
there is that relationship with him alone. That's when I know
what it's all about — or at least enough to keep on going.

Now that is pretty pious language, and I'm sorry about

that, but I don't know what else to use. Perhaps it will help
your students get what I mean if I simply describe how I
came to this position. It's really the experiences of the past
seven years in the ministry that have gotten me this far. The
description has to be somewhat indirect, and it has to do
with two episodes that I take as the symbols of what I am
driving at. One is good; the other is bad. Together they have
given me, I think, some insight.

The good incident is that there has been established a John
B. Coburn Lacrosse Trophy. This has delighted me as nothing
else has these past seven years. It is ironical to think that I
should come to this college to be the chaplain, to represent
the Christian faith, and when I leave, I am memorialized as
the lacrosse coach. That is very fitting and proper.

It is interesting to reflect that in some ways the most personally satisfying and perhaps even the most effective ministry
that I have carried on here has been outside the church and
totally beyond any formal ecclesiastical relationship. I am
just a guy with other guys who happens to know more about
lacrosse than they do, so for two hours every day for two
months we get together, and the most important thing in
our lives is that little ball and how to cradle it and how to
toss it around. We don't have a great team, but it has been
getting better each year, and this year we had four wins to
three losses. The main thing, though, has been the fun we
have all had in it.

It has put me in touch with some real characters, some rare
birds whom I'd never have come to know well otherwise.
Most of them are in the athletic department.

They remind me of my own college days and the place that
the coaches and trainers had there and the impressions they
left upon me. I think that one professor of political theory,
one historian, one lacrosse coach, and one football coach
were the four most important adults in my life there. The
average coach or trainer probably does as much for the
average student as the average professor — at least in terms

of just giving him something to live by and some illustration of what it is to be a human being, rather than simply intellectual.

There is one coach in particular — of soccer — who tells his boys each year: "Remember, boys, this is just a game. Play it as well as you can, and then forget it. Don't take it too seriously. Have some fun. That's the point of what we're doing every afternoon." So they do, and, incidentally — or perhaps not so incidentally — over twenty years the most successful record of any varsity team has been the soccer team.

Another observation I'd make on the basis of lacrosse is that I have noticed each year that the man who is elected captain is seldom the person who began as a freshman with the greatest skill as a lacrosse player. He is always the fellow, rather, who plugs away, comes out on time, does what he is supposed to do, is steady and reliable, though not flashy. The flashy boys have their places, but generally speaking, leadership positions are given to those who are responsible and faithful, rather than those simply with native ability. As I look at life, I think maybe this observation has some bearing elsewhere — maybe everywhere.

Anyway, this lacrosse trophy has come to symbolize, for me, all the fun that there is in natural human associations — having a good time together, gathering around a common enterprise, just simply tossing a ball back and forth with some of the nicest guys. I reflect upon the goodness of life in these associations.

The other incident is just the opposite. That is the bad one. It took place a couple of years ago when a student came in to me and said, "Coburn, you're a real phony."

To say that I was stunned is putting it mildly. I was not only stunned; I was, as the phrase has it, "hurt to the quick."

This was a student I'd known reasonably well. He had been in to see me a few times about the difficulty he was having in getting adjusted to college life. I had been of some help to him and on one occasion had interceded rather strongly with the Dean who, it seemed to me, was being pretty judgmental about this boy. So my associations with him were, on the whole, good, and I liked him.

When he called me a phony, therefore, after I'd taken a deep breath, I asked him if he could give me any reason why he had come to this conclusion.

He replied, "No, just the way you strike me. You don't come through to me except as someone who is something other than you say you are. The other day on the street you said to me, 'How are you?' I knew perfectly well you didn't give a damn how I was. You're putting on a front all the time. If you really want to know how awful I think you are, let me say that when you sat down in the dining hall the other day with that cup of coffee and said you just wanted to talk, I thought I was going to throw up. You may have noticed I couldn't take another cup of coffee — another swallow of coffee, anyway."

Well, there I was. I thought at first that I'd try to reason with this fellow and try to persuade him that I really wasn't such a bad guy after all. All I'd have to do would be to remind him of those nice things I'd done for him.

Then I thought, No, I can't persuade this fellow. There's something inside him that makes it impossible for him to see me as I really am. I'm not all that bad. There's just something inside him, and it may be that he doesn't have any control over it. We just don't click. It's an "I do not like thee, Dr. Fell" kind of thing.

Then I thought to myself, No, that's not quite it either, although that may be accurate. The fact is, he could be right. I may be a phony. Actually, good Lord, I am a phony. Suppose this boy knew me as I really was — just about as phony as you can get. I'm half committed to the Christian faith; I'm proud; I want to get credit for everything that I do; I think other people get credit when I really deserve it; I'm self-centered; I'm lazy. Boy, if he knew me as I know myself to be down inside, then he'd learn what phoniness really means. So perhaps I'd better not argue with him at all.

Of course, if he'd spoken to *you* in the first place, he could have spared himself a lot of trouble. You could have straightened him out about me right at the beginning. You know me as well as anybody and know what a bum I am. And I suppose the best thing about friendship is that you take me as I am anyway. That means a lot. (Besides that, it's a two-way proposition.)

It was just about the same time that a vestryman, with whom I'd always been on good terms and whose mother-in-law I had ministered to during her last days and whose funeral I had taken (quite successfully, I thought), wrote me a letter in which he accused me of trying to take another clergyman's position away from him. The fact was, indeed, quite the opposite — I had gotten that man a position.

I tried to explain this to the vestryman over the telephone. He refused to see me face to face and never answered my letter when I wrote him.

The worst thing about it was that he was such a nice fellow for whom I'd had a genuine affection. He not only didn't trust me anymore; he got other people not to trust me, too, so there was just a nice little network of relationships being broken around me, which ended in my having a real understanding of what the word "isolation" means.

There was something going on in all these relationships — or the breaking of them — that obviously was beyond any rational explanation. What the truth was had no bearing or influence anyway. I was being separated from a group of people whom I'd come to serve and to whom I thought I had been a reasonably faithful pastor.

In a word, I guess you would say I came in touch personally with the power of the evil one. Anyone who says the devil is dead is just crazy. He's still at work underneath the surface of life, all right. The trouble is, I've not only seen what he's done and continues to do, but at some times I have

helped him. During that time it was just as though we were
all caught up in a network out of which we couldn't free
ourselves. That was about as close to hell as I've ever been.

What such an experience does, of course, is to drive you to
your knees. It drove me. Where else was I to go? I couldn't
fight these people. I could argue until I was blue in the
face. I could even tell them the whole story and ask them to
verify it with Almighty God. They just wouldn't have anything to do with it.

All I could do was to try to remain open to those people, to
be faithful to the task I'd been given, to hope that I wouldn't
make the situation worse myself, and then wait. There wasn't
anything else to do except wait, and I mean wait upon the
Lord.

That was when I learned the greatest lesson I think I've
ever learned in prayer because the Lord tossed the thing right
back to me. He said, "You decide what you're going to do
about this. I'll be around to help you, but you've got to make
up your mind. Don't expect me to tell you what to do. You've
got to decide what to do. You can go one way or another. You
can go around feeling sorry for yourself. You can justify yourself (I know you have plenty of reason to do that), or you can
try to be quietly faithful. Stay open to those people. Keep your
mouth closed.

"Then, if that's what you'll do, put it in my hands. Something will happen. You won't have to worry."

Well, that's what I tried to do to the best of my ability. It
was a great lesson. So when I talk about a personal relationship with God, this is what I'm talking about. This has, I think,
put some iron in the bottom of my soul. It taught me not to put
my trust in men — and yet, of course, you do have to put your
trust in men. You have to put your trust in God, and you can
only do this as you stay open to men.

It has been, if I may say so, a hard lesson. I realize that I
really am not much. Believe me, it keeps you humble.

Well, both of these incidents — one good and one evil, neither one really deserved — add up, I think, to one thing. Of course, you have to add thousands of other things that circle around these two poles as well. I think it's summarized in that book, *The Diary of a Country Priest,* by Georges Bernanos, which I read this last year. On the last page the priest, who really has had a pretty tough time in human relationships, sums it all up by saying: " Grace is everywhere." That's just about it.

So, for what it's worth, you can give this to your boys — grace is everywhere. No matter what comes, it can be grace in a personal relationship with God.

All best wishes.

Sincerely,

A Postscript

Well, Jesus, it's true what they say — the best things in life are free, aren't they? The real good things come free of charge — things like love and being forgiven and somebody liking you even if you are a stinker; and sitting around a fire and having a beer and relaxing after you've been on the slopes all day; and having your child say, " Gee, Pops, it's good you're home."

You don't earn any of these gifts. They are sheer grace. They are given. And they're free.

But there is another side to this — the best things cost an awful lot. In fact, you have to pay a terrific cost for some — maybe most — of the best things: like knowing you can trust life after you've been cut down, or falling flat on your face and discovering you can get up again, or losing someone you love and one day having your life move onto another level, and you suddenly discover you're being carried by someone or something, and you don't have to be afraid anymore.

So now there is a question: How come that the most exhilarating experience of all is to pray to you and get no answer because we know you don't exist at all? Why is that so strengthening? Is it because the greatest gift of all is that you trust us

so much we don't even need you? And is that what it's like to
live at our fullest and freest and best — to be without you?
Well, thanks for that, too. That costs us everything — doesn't it?
— like our lives.

So here is this pain I have. Jesus, I don't want to pretend it's
just dandy. I hate it. I hate the pain and I hate the failure and
I hate the mortification. I wish to hell I didn't have it.

But you didn't ever pretend you wanted to suffer either, did
you? You never said in the Garden on that last night, " Dear
Father, thanks ever so much for the cup of suffering. I'd love
to drink it."

No. You said, " Take it away. If you only will, take it away.
But if you won't, if this is really what I must do, if you are to
have your way, then, O.K., I'll do it. But I'm doing it for you —
not for me."

No wonder they call it your agony. You sound just like any
of us agonizing. Of course you were like any of us, humanly
speaking. You were a man.

Yet you were willing to trust that somehow what was your
worst was meant to be God's best and that God could make
it that way. So if it was best for God, then — in faith — it was
best for you.

So then, here. You take this worst of mine. You do something with it. I'll try not to run away from it. I'll try not to
cover up on it. I'll try to stay open to people and keep coming
back to them, no matter what they say or do. I'll try to be
faithful.

If it's for those others that I have been given this, then I'll
stay open to them. I'll try to. But you'll have to help me.

O.K., then. Here it is. It's yours. And mine too, I suppose.

And here are all the good things, too — those gifts I don't
deserve. Those are yours, too. And mine.

All the worst — all the best — and all in between. All life is
grace. Thanks, Jesus. Thanks. Amen.

VIII

A LETTER TO A YOUNGER SON [1]

Cambridge, Mass.
November 23, 1963

Dear Mike:

We have been thinking of you particularly since hearing the tragic news about President Kennedy yesterday. It is beyond belief and yet there it is — something we have to take in, a dreadful event for our country and for all mankind, a terrible loss for Americans and especially for those who felt about him as you did. I am glad you have that letter and signature to keep forever.

Your mother and I have just heard President Johnson declare Monday to be a national day of mourning. That is a great thing to do for all of us not only as a nation but as individuals who have lost someone who is really part of ourselves, the way a President is. It is right to mourn, to grieve and to cry. There have been no dry eyes around here for the past twenty-four hours. I feel a little the way we did when Cynthia died. This seems like a member of the family. There are times when if you cry you are a baby. But not this time. This is what you do when you love somebody and then that person is lost. So I hope you haven't been ashamed to cry.

---

[1] This letter originally appeared in *That Day with God,* ed. by William M. Fine (McGraw-Hill Book Company, Inc., 1965), and is reprinted here with permission of the publishers.

But the crying — this kind of crying is really for ourselves. It helps us. It doesn't help President Kennedy, though it is a tribute to him, and I think that somehow it probably makes him a little proud. He doesn't need our help, though, because now he has God's help and that is all he needs. We've had a lot of talks in this family about life after death and where Cynthia is, and what she's doing, and how she can fly as an angel when she hasn't any arms and all that kind of thing. It's probably good for us to do this once in a while, if we don't take our own ideas too seriously. The fact is of course we can't be certain about any of those details. The only thing we can be certain of is that God is God and everyone with God is safe. So Cynthia is O.K. and President Kennedy is O.K. and so is everybody else who is with God — and that includes us, so long as we are with God. So we can weep all right and it's a good thing for us to do. But we don't have to weep for the President. He's with God and he's all right. As a matter of fact I even believe that some day you can count on seeing him and telling him about your letter. But he will know about it anyway, I suppose. Anyway, seeing President Kennedy is going to be one of the good things about dying. There are a lot of others it's going to be good to see. You can imagine seeing Caesar, for example, so you'd better get moving on that Latin. I'm only kidding, Mike, about the Latin, but a question you might ask your roommate is, "What language do you speak in heaven?" Dr. Guthrie says it's Hebrew, which is going to make it tough for most of us.

There are two other things I want to say about this death. The first isn't pleasant, but it's real and has to be faced honestly sooner or later, so I might as well spell it out now. This is that there is a power of evil at work in the world, and it is an active force against all that is good and lovely and true. You see it when some evil man in an office building kills a President, or when death comes to some innocent baby, or when I lost my temper and knocked you on top of the head, or when I booted Tom in the seat of the pants, or when

people suffer pain the way Professor Batten did, or when
some fellows are lonely all the time and nobody accepts them
or is nice to them, or when wars break out, or when white
people slam doors in the face of Negroes, or when big kids
tease and beat up little kids. There is something going on
that is evil in the world, and it's got a lot of power.

And what is worse, some of it gets into all of us. We can't just
separate people into the " good guys " and the " bad guys."
There is something of both good and bad in all men, including nice people like you and me, and it is this mixture that
makes life and its different battles so complicated.

Now the other thing I want to say is that this power of evil,
strong as it is at times, and apparent victor every once in a
while as when the President is shot — this power of evil does
not have the last word. Love does. Decency does. Truth does.
Honor does. Not cheating on an examination does. Giving
your life for your country in time of war does. Keeping your
temper does. Keeping your word even when it is to your advantage not to does.

In one word, God is more powerful than everything set
against him. And I'm using the word " God " now in the biggest
sense possible, as that force in the universe which is responsible for all creation, which undergirds all man's discoveries,
and which calls us all to a life of nobility, or honesty, if a
less fancy word is better, and service. And if I had to add it all
up I'd say that this is the life which was in Jesus of Nazareth.
Stick around him, trying to live with his spirit, ask God for
his help by praying, and gradually all the disjointed bits of
life begin to fall into place. Friendship is more fundamental
than loneliness, life than death, and love than hate, because
all of this is the character of God.

What this means for all of us, I guess, right now is that we
don't get discouraged or afraid or give up hope. We know
that we are on the right track because President Kennedy
really was " a great and good man," as President Johnson just
called him. And his greatness and goodness were from God

and cannot therefore ever die.

So all Americans can respond to the best that is in them now because this is a great and good country — not because it is ours but because it is God's. And we can make it more God's now than ever before as all of us in some small way become a little greater and a little better ourselves. That means I have to be a better dean than I've ever been, and a better father and husband. And you have to be a better student. I won't say a better son, because you're a good one now.

I won't say you're a good student. Your mother and I were pleased with the last marks because you weren't flunking anything, but we agree with you that they weren't great and that you can do better. So get on the stick and work at those books — not really for our sakes, though you know we'd be pleased, but for the sake of all of us in this country, and for J.F.K. and all he stands for, and for God because he is as ready to help you as he is those who now live with him forever, and of course for your own sake.

Well, I don't want to turn this into a sermon, though I must confess you've always been kind in your remarks about my sermons, and I appreciate it. I really just want you to know we are thinking of you, and we love you, and wish you well as a person living and growing up in a great and good country in a great and good generation to be alive.

It will be wonderful to have you home for Thanksgiving. We are planning to meet your cousins late in the day and then go see the Bruins play (I think) the Rangers. The poor Bruins are having a miserable season and need our help. Judy will be home for dinner, but has to return to school that night. Tom will meet us at the Cape on Friday with Sue.

We hope all goes well these next few days. Sarah sends her love. So does your mother. So do I. God bless you.

Love,

A LETTER TO FRIENDS

Cambridge, Mass.
July 8, 1966

Dear Jane and Fred:

You have been much on my mind these last days. I am more grateful than I can say for your getting in touch with me and then especially for those good two hours together. It was fine that at the end we could all — with the children — sit around and finish the salmon salad. That was a mysterious sacramental meal in which we shared — family, friends, Jamie, and the Spirit of our Lord. Wasn't it nice to have that Fourth of July salmon left over? You are good patriots.

I really don't want to say anything I haven't already said. There isn't, in a sense, anything more to say. There is no accounting for that accident. It doesn't make any sense. Nobody was to blame — and even if there was, what would that prove? It was just a senseless, accidental, sudden gust of wind and the capsizing of the boat.

Yet I must put in writing my own conviction that you will see Jamie again. Oh, I don't know how — in what form, with what eyes, or any of that. I just know that he, as a son, and you, as parents, will be in a relationship where you recognize each other and can affirm each other and be glad in each other, and that you will be carried in a spirit that death can't destroy. The last word, in other words, isn't that Jamie is dead, but that in Christ he is alive and that you, who belong to each other in Christ, will be in touch with each other.

I don't know what you'll do. Maybe you'll just say, " Hi! " But I think that you will be so caught up in an eternal spirit that simply *is* all of existence that you won't worry about that. There will simply be an abiding sense of rightness and peace and strength. We'll go zooming around because our true selves will be let loose and we'll be able to be ourselves fully

— that is, really love without ourselves getting in the way.

Did you ever have the experience of running along the beach and running and running and running and never getting winded or pooped, and it seemed as though you could just keep going forever? I think that's something of what it's going to be like. There will be inexhaustible energy just for being — that is, for loving — because we'll be our best selves.

Or, since you are sailors, maybe the figure to use is when you are running before the wind and you let out the spinnaker and suddenly the wind takes hold; you get lifted on top of the waves, and then you just skim along. There is no fighting against the wind, no battling the waves against the boat. Everything is together. Every inch of sail is being used; the waves are with you rather than against you; everything is going for you; you just are in it all and carried by it; and you have the sense of just about taking off. It's glorious; just sheer glory.

So it's with that in the background that we keep going on in the foreground where we're living. Life is going to go on. We are meant to go on, too. We can't hang back waiting for something or someone to come along and give us a push so we get started again. No, we have to get going ourselves — get to work at 8:30, get the children off and the dishes done, pay the bills, stay on the school board, and all the rest.

It's just that now we do it all within a different dimension, and in some way with a different purpose, or at least with a deeper understanding of what it's all about, and so with a gentleness we haven't had before. Gentleness and strength. I guess that's about what I mean. Maybe that's grace.

One thing I am very sorry about. When I left after lunch, I walked out of the house without saying good-by to Mary. That was awful of me. I know how important someone in that place is: behind the scenes, fixing meals, washing the dishes, keeping an eye on the children — just being there. Sometimes I think people like Mary are the cement that holds the whole structure of life together — just because she goes about doing what she always does, but now with a grief and a sadness for

Jamie and for the whole family. That's spiritual work if I've ever seen any. Her tears shall be turned to joy.

Tell her that, will you? And tell her I'm sorry I was so thoughtless as just to walk out and not say "hello" to her.

Don't answer this. Just remember I love you. We both love you. Everybody loves you. So does God. That's what it's about.

Love,

A Postscript

So, Jesus of Nazareth, let me not worry about whether I am joyful or peaceful or hopeful or not.

Just let me be content to trust you and to do what I think you want me to do.

Don't let me have a clear idea of what you want me to do — and then let it slide by. That's death, and I know it because I've done it often enough.

If I can keep sound inside — trusting and obeying — then I know I'll get carried by life — or by you — and that will give me all the happiness I'll need.

I'll be with it. Or I'll be with you. That will be enough.

So help me to be faithful to what I already know.

You are the Lord.

And now let me mention those who have gone on from this life into the resurrected life with you. Remember me to them. I know that all is well with them, for you are their Lord.

And ours. Thank you. Amen.

IX

A LETTER TO A COLLEGE SENIOR

Cambridge, Mass.
May 2, 1965

Dear Dick:

Thank you for your letter and for the honor of asking me my opinion about the ministry and whether you should seriously consider going into it.

Well, yes, I think you should seriously consider it. You are intelligent; you have interest in things of the mind. You are concerned about social issues, else you would not have gone on the march from Selma to Montgomery, and you have cared enough about people to give a few hours a week to the tutorial program. The instincts that you have as a human being are sound and good, and they are the kind called for in the ministry.

You are the kind of person who likes to get involved in discussions about the meaning of life and of art and culture and drama and sex and everything that goes into making up the human enterprise. If you are trying to find out what gives all across the board of the human scene, without necessarily buying the traditional Christian interpretation (I'll come to that later), then you have the broad human interests that can be a base for the ministry. In other words, you are a reasonably mature human being concerned about the human enterprise, and that is enough for considering the ministry.

When you ask the question, " But what about the darned old church? " you ask exactly the right question. That's just where the rub is: can you make your life count for more — or for less — by tying it up with " the darned old church "? Don't think the question gets any easier to answer as you get older. A bishop friend of mine says, " Every morning I have to make up my mind all over again whether I'll stick with it or not."

Unless you are quite different from your contemporaries, you've probably been through — or are still in — a healthy period of revolt against the church, its conservatism, its anti-intellectualism, its stodginess, its concern with picayune issues, its failure to provide clear leadership on social issues, and a thousand and one other things.

But since you've asked me directly the question about the ministry, I gather you are like a number — not a great but a significant number — of young people who wonder, perhaps wistfully, if a life can't count more in the long run in the church than anywhere else. All I can say is that for some people, yes.

For you, I don't know. But let me clarify a few matters, or at least comment on them.

The first thing is about " the call." The way this has been put traditionally is: " Have you a call from God to go into the ministry or don't you? If you do, then you'd better go, and if you don't get the call, don't go."

This idea has fouled up so many people that I have about decided the best advice I can give is forget it. *Any* idea of the call can get you so off balance that it does more harm than good. So you'd be better off if you took any idea of the call you have and just throw it away.

It's better to start from scratch — that is, just like everybody else. On one level, there is nothing fundamentally different in a man's going into the ministry from going into teaching or medicine or business or whatever else. The essential questions are the same: What are his abilities and interests as a person? What possibilities does the profession have for him? Can he

do the work required? What does he want to do? Is there a
social need that is met by the profession? Well, make up your
mind and then do it.

You make up *your* mind on the basis of *your* experiences
and *your* understanding of *yourself* and *your* God and then
go do it.

In other words, you are a human being. You have the responsibility as a free man — a free *Christian* man — to make a
free choice. For Pete's sake, be a man, then, and decide. Don't
expect somebody else to decide for you — no father, or teacher,
or priest, or friend, or voice from a cloud. *You* decide. To be
able to take all the evidence in, weigh it, and then make a free
decision — that is the mark of a mature man, and of a mature
Christian man.

Well, you may say, "I don't have enough evidence." And
that is part of the problem. You're twenty-one years old. You
are just graduating from college. You didn't do any significant
work until your junior year. You still are not sure what life is
all about. So my second point is: go get some experience. Then
you'll have something to go on to decide, some raw material
for the spirit to work on.

Just get some nice, honest, human experience — like a job
from nine to five. Just like everyone else. See how life really
is for 95 percent of the people — quite different from class-
rooms, fraternities, beer parties, and football games, not that
there is anything the matter with any of those things. It's just
that they don't (particularly when your old man is paying for
them) provide you with enough natural human experiences to
help you decide what to do with your life — certainly not
enough for the ministry. You're not tough enough to make that
decision now.

So go do something. Get a job. Any job. A Peace Corps job.
A nice job in the Army. Lots of young men have nice and not
so nice jobs in the Army. Why deprive yourself of such a nice
human experience by going to a graduate school? You won't
learn nearly as much about life — about what it is to be a per-

son — there as you will in the Army.

If you do not like the Army for conscientious reasons and would classify yourself as a pacifist, just go do something conscientious to give expression to that concern. Go work with the Quakers or the Mennonites or people who do act on their deepest convictions. Do not just hang around grousing, but be a responsible grouser.

Don't take a church job. You will get caught too soon and think the church or its program is central. It's not. Life is central. People are central. God is central.

If you take this second point seriously, I think you will come, in two or three or four or five years, to know what you ought to do with your life. Gradually, it may "come" to you that you are the kind of fellow who can go into the ministry and do a decent job and that you want to do it. *That* is your call. You can't make it in a vacuum, but only on the basis of experience. As you come to know yourself and others, you come to know God, and then you have something to go on because you are going into his service if you go into the ministry, and you have to have some idea of him. The conviction will (probably) grow slowly, and when it comes, it comes out of your experience with people and with God — and knowledge of both.

Well, you will say — or your minister will say — "but isn't the Bible and history filled with young men who have a direct call from God to go serve him? Can't young men today hear that same call at sixteen as well as twenty-six?"

The answer is: yes, of course the Bible and history show that young men have had a sense of being called by God and have served him faithfully. And also, of course, there are some men today aged sixteen who have a deep conviction that they are called by God, respond to that call, and become faithful ministers. I would not want to deny that.

These are, however, exceptions today. In this matter as in baseball, the law of averages pays off in the long run. Casey Stengel was a great baseball manager because he played the law of averages. His *genius* was in knowing when to break it, but he wouldn't have been a genius if he hadn't played most of the games, day in and day out, according to the averages.

The law of averages since World War II, when men went into the ministry after war experiences, is clear: the best men in the ministry are the men with experience outside the ministry. And speaking of illustrations from the Bible and history, I'd point to Paul, Augustine, and St. Francis as the kind of men we need most of all. They kicked around a good deal before they heard a call. Then something beyond " came to them " and they said, Yes. The call arose out of their experiences.

Another thing I want to say: don't be overly concerned about motivation. If you wait around until you are certain you have perfectly clear motives before deciding, you will never decide. There is no such animal. At least there is no such state of human perfection reached that men act only out of love for another or for God.

It's a mixed bag. Some good reasons and some not so good. You want to serve, certainly; but you also (probably) want to be known as someone who serves. You would like to help people, but it gives you a nice sense of superiority when you do help them. You want to convert people, and then you count your conversions.

But this is the way it is meant to be — a mixed bag. This is our human situation. We need to hear again that parable of Jesus about the wheat and the tares. Don't try to pull them apart now, he says. If you try to rip up all the weeds that are so entangled with the wheat, you'll rip up the wheat, too. They are part of the same bundle of life. Let life, in the long run, do the separating. Or — if you prefer — let God in the long run do the separating.

Besides which, your understanding of your motivation will change. What you think are the reasons you did something today, you will come to see five years from now were actually quite different. So don't count on either pure motives or clear understanding of motives. They are mixed, and they change.

You just have to accept this as you are and look at the work to
be done and then simply get going.

What you are asked to do is not to concentrate on purifying
yourself, but to put your trust in God and live as fully as you
know how as a Christian now. If you do that now in this chap-
ter of your life, you will know what to do when the next one
is about to begin. That, incidentally, is part of the fun of being a Christian — you never know what's ahead; all you know
is that if it's for God and under him, then it's going to be all
right and better than you can imagine.

It is somewhat in vogue now to refer to the minister or priest
as the " clown." He comes into life in an absurd fashion. What
can he do? Nothing. Nothing really useful like earning a living and making a contribution to society and really counting
for something.

This is a good figure to use, some people say, because the
fact is that there really isn't much " good " that a minister does
in terms of action. His value is in what he represents, or what
his office represents.

By just being a priest or minister, he points to the absurdity
of life as most of us live it. We take life so seriously, when actually it is more of a joke than anything else. It doesn't amount
to much; we can't make much sense of it; when all our efforts
of three score years and ten (or three score in an affluent society) are added up, they prove very little.

So a " clown " points this out. He makes us laugh at ourselves. He gives us a little perspective. He reminds us that
God plays games, too, and his best game was in creating life
and then watching — sometimes helping — men play their own
games.

Yet, of course, underneath the funny man who makes people laugh there is the tragic figure, the one who weeps. The
absurdity of existence is that love is not returned equally, justice never gets fully established. Once the scales get balanced,
something or someone comes along and tips them over, and
you have to begin all over again. Our noble instincts never re-

main in control for long; the demonic ones surge up and carry us off — at least for a spell.

When man does find love entering his life, frequently it is too much for him to bear. It's tough sometimes just to be loved by someone. Holiness is a scary thing to face. So when love incarnate walks around, he gets spit on and hooted at and then whipped and killed. He is unbearable.

That's tragedy. So Christ is the tragic figure, and all who bear his yoke are tragic figures, too. They are clowns.

Christ is an affront. So is the priest. So is the minister. They remind people that the life they live for the most part — the money grubbing and the drive for status and all the rest — is perfectly foolish. It doesn't mean a thing. They are offended by this reminder.

The clown, in other words, always comes into the circus tent. He pokes fun at the absurdities of life. People laugh at him. Children shriek at his tricks, but when he climbs up and sits next to them, they are scared. He never can come in and sit down and become a member of the audience the way you can imagine the bareback rider doing — or the trapeze artist or the girl who jumps into the tank on horseback. They are all really normal people underneath, just like us. They have developed a special skill, but other than that they're just folks.

Not the clown. He is something different. There is another quality about him entirely. He comes from another world. His very existence both makes us laugh and puts our nerves on edge. Live with him? No thanks.

So, don't ever think you can avoid this if you go into the ministry. Oh, you can moderate the offensiveness; you can be a good guy; you can break through this kind of image from time to time; you can be met by some people as a person; you can have some warm human friendships. But you can never shed the clown from your being entirely, because that is what you become — or what the priesthood or ministry chosen by you always sets before people: laugh and cry. That's life, brother, laugh and cry. Laugh until you cry. And when you've cried enough, then look up — your Lord and Savior draws nigh.

It's laughter and crying, fun and games and pain, goodness and demons all together. Look, if you want to embrace the whole of existence — the absurdities and tragedies, laced with satisfactions and laughs — where better than the priesthood?

You remember that I said earlier to forget any idea of "the call" and make up your mind the way anybody does. While it is perfectly true that on one level you do have to make a decision just the way anybody would in deciding, for example, to become a dentist, on another level it isn't like that at all. This deeper level is where you are playing for keeps; all the chips are down, out there on the table, and you have to bet. You have to bet your life. You have to bet your life on what the hell you think is going on in life and in the world. And you can't play it safe.

Well, I'll tell you. No, that's presumptuous. I don't *know* what's going on — in the sense that I know $2 + 2 = 4$ and that the Red Sox are not going to win the pennant this year. But I have faith that gives me stuff to go on, and it's that knowledge that I'm pointing to now. That faith is that right now, before our very eyes, right in all the things that we do, right in the hate and the pain and the wars and the social conflicts, God is working. He is trying to get some kind of social order that will make these riots and wars and terrific imbalances between rich nations and poor out of the question. He is already here, and he is at work in every place where there is some kind of fellowship being developed and mutuality and trust and sympathy being established. Wherever justice is emerging, he is at work; wherever restrictive covenants are being broken, he is breaking them; wherever comfort is given and man's spirit strengthened and compassion set loose, he is — as they say — working his purpose out.

"Well," you may reply, "all you are saying is that people are doing these things." Precisely. People are doing them. How else do you think God gets things done? He can't do anything except through people. Some are Christian people; most aren't.

That, from one point of view, doesn't make the slightest difference. What matters is whether justice and love are becoming greater possibilities in society and in personal lives or less. Can the Negro buy a house next to you or can't he? Did you take a stand in your fraternity against excluding boys on grounds of race or not? Did you honor the honor system or did you chicken out when you saw your house president cheat? These are the questions that count.

So the church. Here's "your darned old church." Let me hit this just as hard as I can. That's what the church is for.

Let me go further. That's what the church does. It is now bearing God (or Christ, if you want to be theologically technical) into society and into the lives of people. Or, rather, since God is already at work in the world, it is trying to meet him there and help him. It's already at work. Already it is helping society and bringing health rather than sickness; already it's setting men free and bringing into being a new social order; already it bears compassion and forgiveness.

"Who is doing this?" you ask. Well, people. Who else is there? Christian people. People who have been given a Christian name, who are fighting a fight in behalf of the one who gave it to them, who are at work in the world doing whatever it is they are meant to be doing — raising children, selling groceries, building bridges, kicking footballs. They may do it well or ill, but the point is that there in the world in them Christ is at work in and through all the structures of life and of society. How else can Christ get there?

Now, I am not saying that Christian people are doing God's work and non-Christians aren't. That would be foolish, and everybody knows lots of non-Christians who act in a more Christian way than many Christians. But what I am saying is that Christians know what they are about (or ought to). They know they are the Lord's and are about his business. And so are *all* men — they are the Lord's, too. Christians can help them come to know this, but they do it only by working in the world side by side with them.

Therefore, and here is the conclusion: the church is at the heart of social reconstruction and personal renewal. Or Christ is at the heart of it, and this is the same thing. This constant, persistent, year after year, generation after generation of being in life and affirming by one's own life that Christ is the Lord of life — this is what the church is doing. It is what the church is. To remind Christian people who they are, so that all men may know who they are — that is the reason for the church. They are the Lord's. They may not know it, the Lord knows that, too. The church's purpose is to be the church — Christian people, to be Christian people — so that the world and all the nations therein may acknowledge in peace and justice that the Lord he is God.

No, I'm not talking simply about the institutional church. That is, I am in part — the church, after all, is a historic institution with big cathedral buildings and budgets and run-down property and underpaid employees and all that. But I am talking about the inner reality of the church that is known by faith, that is one with Christ, and therefore is one church (despite the obvious visible, institutional differences) and within which the whole meaning of human existence is caught up and affirmed.

It's known in people's living and suffering and dying and being raised up again, and getting on with the job and getting a kick out of life — its absurdities and tragedies — and being joyful in the whole enterprise. The Biblical word is *joyful* in the Lord. That means that the whole package deal is right and good and fun and great. So don't settle for little snippets of good things like too much food and too much sex and too much drink and too much money in the bank. That's kid stuff. Settle for the wholeness of life — buy the full package. That means to be able to take it all in and live it.

I honestly don't see — and here I am confessing my personal faith — how you can do this unless you get close to Christ, get inside and see what he is all about. That means to be in that Spirit which lives, gets killed, comes back, and keeps on living, and which always tries to reconcile and to love. It is what it means to be baptized into the death of Jesus that we may be partakers of his resurrection — and, therefore, to live with power, all out, so to speak. You do it as you trust Christ and try to obey him. That's where the secret lies.

Anyway, this is what the church is about. This is the reason the church is in business. This is what the business of the priesthood and ministry is: to keep this before people, helping them live what they already are.

Don't tell me you don't see evidences of this in your church at home, that you have an idiot for a minister and nothing but hypocrites in the congregation, or that there is a lot of bad stuff that goes on there. I know all about it. Anything you know that's bad, I know doubled in spades. It's worse even than you think. " The darned old church " is a real problem.

But that's not the point. The point is inside; it is at the heart of the church's life. Hidden away beneath and in all the mustiness and self-will and struggle for power and even evil, there is the Spirit of the living Lord. He is hidden, to be sure. But he is expressed from time to time in the lives of people. He comes forth in the sacramental life of those people — hidden there, too. Still, if he is everywhere, he must be somewhere and he is there most of all. That — all that is represented there — is the Bread of Life.

Now, making this possible for people is the business of priests. So if you want — when all is said and done — if you really want to count for people on the very deepest, darkest, most glorious levels of their existence, then consider — and I just say " consider " — the ministry.

But for right now, don't worry too much about the ministry itself. Just go be a human being somewhere. What is important is that you go get mixed up with life, that is, with other human beings. That is the best way to get mixed up with God. In fact, it's the only way. Then in that mixture of your self with other selves and with God, you will come to know whether it is right for you to go into the ministry or not.

So go hang around people doing the work of the world for a while. That's where God is. Then, in time, it will come to you what to do. That may be a call to go into the ministry; or it may be a call to do something else. At that juncture, what is important is not being a minister (or a dentist). What is important is that you do that which you believe is right under God for you to do.

So you decide. Then do it. That's all. Keep me in touch. With all best wishes.

Sincerely,

A Postscript

So, Jesus of Nazareth, just help me do a good job where I am. No, that is not enough, help me do the very best job of which I am capable. If you have given me an assignment, let me carry it out to the best of my ability.

Let me not worry whether it is church work or not. If it's your work, then that's enough.

Let the teacher be the best teacher he can be. Let the wife concentrate on making her husband as happy as she knows how; let her comfort him. Let him be concerned about her happiness rather than his own and set her free from himself, so that she may be fully expressing all the gifts she has been given.

Let the salesman sell with loyalty to his product and no under-the-counter deals; and the manufacturer give him a product that is what is claimed for it; and the workman take pride in producing his day's work.

For it is this kind of daily living, this carrying out of society's assignments, that reflects our loyalty to you; for society is to serve man; and our service is in carrying out the work you have given us to do.

This is how your hidden work gets done when we do it in your Spirit and for your purposes.

May my Christian life be, then, not so much a taking on of

extra assignments in the church world, but carrying out with a pure intention and as well as I can the assignments in the world I already have. As I can, help me to recollect your presence as I do your work. But most of all, help me to do your work.

Lest I be content with accepting in a passive spirit too limited a responsibility, may I go among your people — especially where the lines are drawn and conflict is breaking — to serve as one who is content to be there and to serve. For if I am not there, how can your service be done through me? Keep calling me, then, O Lord. May I not forget that your call to stay is usually more difficult to heed than the call to go.

Jesus of Nazareth, great is your name, and your glory spreads throughout the heavens and even in the heart of man. May I live in your Spirit and share in your glory now and just where I am. Amen.

X

A LETTER TO AN OLDER SON

Order of the Holy Cross
West Park, New York
August 3, 1966

Dear Tom:

During these past few days at Holy Cross, you have been much on my mind as I have been recapitulating some of the experiences of my own life and thinking of the new life on which you are about to embark. As you know, I think what you are going to do is just exactly right.

I do not believe you will ever regret this decision to take the job in Beirut. There will be times, no doubt, when things go wrong, or you have a touch of homesickness. We never outgrow that fully, I think; there is a pang in drawing away from that which is familiar and where we belong. You notice it especially when you are on a train pulling out of a station at the beginning of a long trip, or on a ship setting out across the ocean. Dr. Jung has some profound insights here. At some moments you will wonder why you ever took the job, but those will pass. The overwhelming conviction that will be yours, I don't doubt at all, will be that this has been one of the crucial steps in your life and will mark a real turning point.

In what way it will cause you to turn, of course, I haven't the faintest idea. In one sense, it is none of my business, and in another, it doesn't make any difference. What does make the difference is that it be your direction that you choose; and whatever way is right for you on your terms and in your way is right. All I would want is that you walk step by step to cover your own ground, and that when you come to know what it is you want to do, you do it freely and with your whole heart and have some fun doing it.

You might as well be warned, though, that in some measure the cards are stacked against you. You remember meeting last Christmas that Mike Coburn (no relation) who came to Judy's party? This spring his father, John Coburn (also no relation), lent me the Coburn genealogy. You are the twelfth generation of Coburns in this country. The first three were farmers. All the rest — with the exception of your great-grandfather who was a doctor — were either teachers or preachers, or both. To what extent we are really free agents in life is a good question. Maybe, despite all the agonizing each of us has to go through, the pattern is pretty determined anyway.

Feel free to break it, of course. Knock it to smithereens if that helps you find your own way. But, in any case, for what it is worth, this is part of your heritage. The psalmist speaks of a goodly heritage, and I guess that is fair enough for us, too.

There is both a sadness and a gladness that your mother and I feel about your going. The sadness is that, of course, we shall miss you. You are a good egg. We have enjoyed your company simply as a fellow human being. You have done a good job with your life. It has been almost too good, and you have been almost too responsible. Perhaps you should have fallen flat on your face sometime. But I guess I needn't worry about that — you will. It happens to all of us sometime or other. And that's a good lesson. But we don't have to do it deliberately. That will come. All we are asked to do is just what you've done — carried out your different assignments and responsibilities (and honors) as they have come to you.

So we shall miss you for all *that* as well as the fact that you are our son. That's very personal and with only one side of our nature. We hate to see you go.

But with another side we don't at all. It's time you struck out for yourself — and nothing will do that better than getting your body five thousand miles away from here and getting submerged in a totally new life, in a different culture, and where you simply have to deliver some goods. So, from this point of view, we see you go with a great deal of enthusiasm.

To be perfectly honest, I must confess I do get a kick out of seeing you go through an experience somewhat similar to my own. I know that this is for all the bad reasons — living your life over again in your son — but I hope it is more than that. It's just that that kind of life meant so much to me that I hope you get something of the same excitement and satisfaction. Besides that, it was out there that I met your mother, so you ought to be thankful!

That leads me to observe that you seem to be having as much trouble with your girls as I did. I'm certainly not going to give you any advice. As a matter of fact, I should have kept my mouth shut more than I have.

I just want to say this: you choose the girl you want to for the reasons that seem good to you — and if you want to tell me to go to hell, that's all right with me. You know me well enough to know that I'm probably going to make some comment or other anyway. After all, there's no point in my pretending I don't have a point of view about girls — both in general and in particular. It would be pretty stupid to go through life completely neutral on that subject. Anyway, be that as it may, I just want to be sure you get this straight from me — you make your choice; it's your life; and whatever choice you make is O.K. with me. Don't be under any idea that you ought to be influenced by my judgments. At least not because they're mine. You might, of course, be influenced by the wisdom in those judgments. You can see how wise I am by observing the choice I finally made in your mother. (I'm only kidding. I'm not smart enough. God did it. Or your mother. Or, I guess — down deep — it was all three of us.)

So go your merry way. Keep your eyes open and have a

good time. I just hope the Lord does get in it somewhere along the line; but that's up to you and him, not me.

I don't think I have much else to say. There is no point in my getting off one of my " heart to heart " talks. I can just hear you saying with a patient note of exasperation, " Yes, Father."

But I think I will say this word, because I might not have a chance to say it again. I might be dead or something before you come back. Besides, I'd probably never say it to you face to face. Therefore, better in writing.

I just hope you come to forgive me as you go along in life. I'm not asking you to do anything or say anything — or write anything. I am just expressing the hope that as you get off on your own and begin to come to grips with life, you will in the process come to accept me and forgive me for all the bum things — things done and not done — that I have been responsible for.

Now the strange thing is that, as I ransack my memory, I can't find a great number of actions I have performed that have been so awful. There's sin for you! I'll bet you could remind me of a few. Yes, we'll never forget kicking you up the stairs in Newark (but I did come all the way back from downtown to tell you that I was sorry!). I'm sure I've put pressure on you when it was all wrong, and I've been a little too eager for you to see things my way rather than urging you — really *urging* you — to see how you looked at things. It's that old problem of trying to remake others in our own image — to play God. That, I guess, is the main problem. We all try to do it, but it's especially tough on a son growing up when his old man does it to him.

Anyway, it's that, I guess, more than anything else which I ask your forgiveness for. It's a kind of forgiveness for what I am more than anything else. And when a son can do that for a father, a great step forward has been taken — by the son as well as the father.

I know. It took me years to forgive my father.

Well, that's about it. There was a nice passage read last

night at supper by one of the monks in that book you suggested be read, *Creative Brooding*, by Robert Raines. An adopted son is trying to thank his foster parents for what they have given him, and the father objects by quoting a saying, " The love of parents goes to their children, but the love of these children goes to *their* children." Then he says in effect, " Don't worry about paying us back with love; just pass it on."

I like that. Just pass on whatever love your mother and I have given you, and your life will be all right.

Now one favor. On your first night in Paris will you please walk along the Pont Neuf and sit down for a few minutes on one of the stone benches in those little alcoves near the statue of Henri IV with your back to Notre Dame? Then offer a little prayer for your mother and me, Judy, Mike, and Sarah, and, of course, anyone else you have a mind to.

Then walk back along the Seine on the left bank until you come to the street that runs to your left directly in front of the entrance to Notre Dame. To your right, across the street, is a little bistro. Go in and order a " sandwich jambon." Then tell me what they give you.

Bon voyage. We all love you. And have a *good* time.

Love,

A *Postscript*

So, Jesus of Nazareth, this is a great mixed-up bag of tricks you've given us for this life — good and bad, laughs and tears, birth and death, hate and love, walking away and coming back, you and man. Gifts come that we do not deserve, and blows we don't deserve either. Except, maybe, the latter we do; for, though not perhaps in any neat historical sequence of cause and effect, we do deserve to get knocked down when we try to play God. When don't we? Not so much in our actions, perhaps — just in our spirit and attitude. You're God, or the Son of God. We're not; we're men. That is our glory. So let us be men. But not pretend we're God. When life clips us, that is a good reminder. Thanks for that way of telling us what it is to be a man.

Thanks for carrying us. Or thanks for letting life carry us. It's the same thing, isn't it? When we trust it, we go along. When we distrust it, we fight it. We fight it and ourselves and other people and you. How come you have to trust life and believe in it and let yourself go to find out what it's all about? When we do that, then we can affirm it, say it's good, glad to be alive, and all the rest.

But only as we obey you. That's too bad, Jesus, about that obedience. That rubs us the wrong way. Why can't we move along in life, trusting it and you and people and having a good time affirming everything, and let it go at that? Just because that's not the way it is? There is good and evil, right and wrong, honor and dishonor. And our allegiance to them makes a difference.

O.K., then — obedience. But it's not the tightening up of our wills and a stiff upper lip and a determined resolution to do better or knock off that habit or take on some extra burdens. That's not it.

It's letting you do it. Helping you do it. Or your spirit. It's quiet and gradual. It's under the surface, hidden for the most part. It's willing to let love come in and do it, and not insisting on getting our own way. It's setting other people free, not running their lives. It's keeping oneself open to love. Isn't that more like it? That crucifies the old man, all right. That breaks the will to be oneself selfishly. That is a nice gentle, steady corrosion of a man's self into yourself. All right, that's too extreme, but you know what we mean — you quietly take over. You don't hammer your way into our hearts, trying to chisel an entrance through that stony material. It's, rather, just your insistent gentleness, like a nice, easy, constant rain that gradually soaks in, gentle but always there, never giving up, always coming back. What is so powerful as this, Jesus of Nazareth, except God himself?

And *that's*, then, what carries us — a working through life in response to you in love where we can, and in justice when we can't simply love. That is the cross, and you're doing most of the carrying for us. Indeed, you do carry us. Well, life carries us; we don't have to carry it. You carry us, and we're going on our journey ahead.

So the glory that comes, the glory that comes in little snitches and spots, blurred and murky, but then once in a while clear, crisp, holy, that breaks through, or bursts onto the surface or is seen in the depths — that glory is you. That is your Kingdom. It is in that which lives in the world of men, hidden, and in which we live by faith, which has come to bless us and this world. You have come, the Lord of the living and the dead, of this world and the world to come, for today and forever.

Jesus of Nazareth — it's great. You are great. Thanks. Amen.

PART TWO

AN INTRODUCTION TO CONTEMPORARY SPIRITUALITY

XI

ON THE SPIRITUAL AND THE HUMAN

The theme of this book is that the spiritual life for contemporary man can best be understood in terms of human life and ordinary human experiences. The framework within which this point of view is expressed clearly is that oft-quoted phrase of Dietrich Bonhoeffer's:

> To be a Christian does not mean to be religious in a particular way, to cultivate some particular form of asceticism (as a sinner, a penitent or a saint), but to be a man. It is not some religious act which makes a Christian what he is, but participation in the sufferings of God in the life of the world.[1]

The spiritual life, therefore, is involvement in the human situation, for it is this which leads to " participation in the sufferings of God in the life of the world." Christian spirituality is a Christian style of living.

When we talk of the spiritual life, we are talking of human life and of the spirit which directs that life. It can be put as sharply as this: the spirit of the living God dwells in human life, shaping human society for twentieth-century man, or he does not dwell anywhere. If he does not live in our lives, our flesh, our loves, our failures, our societies, and our victories,

---

[1] Dietrich Bonhoeffer, *Prisoner for God: Letters and Papers from Prison,* ed. by Eberhard Bethge, tr. by Reginald H. Fuller (The Macmillan Company, 1954), p. 166.

then he is dead. Or, if he is not dead, he might as well be.

The first part of this book consists primarily of letters. They are very ordinary letters concerned with the natural, normal experiences of a man whose only virtue is that he belongs to the twentieth century. Their purpose is to make it clear that spiritual experiences are human experiences and that they are related to a man's own times. What makes a man spiritual is his participation in the events of his day because that is where God's Spirit is.

To what extent is the human spirit the bearer of God's spirit? How can looking at a twentieth-century man lift our eyes to see *the* man? Can the new man be discerned through the eyes of the old? In our concern for our day and for the men of our day, what shall we make of him who was "the man for others" in another day? How shall we regard Jesus of Nazareth?

It is not easy for contemporary man to make anything of him. Two thousand years ago is a long time. It is so far back in another age that it is practically out of this world. Nine tenths of all scientists in the history of the world are living today. Nine tenths of scientific knowledge has been discovered within the present generation. What was known two thousand years ago (or twenty, for that matter) has, for the most part, turned out to be not very reliable. In any case, what has been discovered scientifically since the beginning of the twentieth century exceeds in sheer amount everything discovered in all the previous centuries.

Furthermore, while the Gospels are not meant to present a historical biography of Jesus, they are, nevertheless, filled with historical references. The relationship of these "faith documents" to historical "facts" confuses modern man.

It is clear that the accounts are referring to events that took place in the eastern Mediterranean, in a particular historical period when the histories of the Roman state and the Jewish people were intertwined. They are centered in one Jesus of Nazareth, who is a historical figure. He is not, however, known simply as a man of history. He is known by faith as the Lord of all history. He did indeed walk the earth as Jesus of Nazareth, but his Lordship is seen in his resurrection from the dead — during the time of Pontius Pilate — and *that* is seen by the eyes of faith through the power of his Spirit, which is given to those who believe.

The Gospels proclaim this event. It took place in Christ. Once we put ourselves by faith within the event, then we can begin to see God's purpose in history from the beginning to the end — his plan of salvation. It is this proclamation which is the gospel (kerygma). It says something about God's acts in Christ, which are the key to the meaning of history and, therefore, of men's lives personally and in society.

This relationship of faith to history is not easy for "scientific" man to understand. It may help simply to comment that we are not called as modern men to search anxiously for the "historical" Jesus. The details of the historical situations described in the Gospels may be less, rather than more, accurate in many instances. Whether it was five thousand who were fed or twenty-two or none; whether Jesus literally walked on the water or only seemed to; whether water actually was turned into wine — all such questions are of no *fundamental* importance. What is central in all such incidents as these is that Jesus of Nazareth is set forth as the Lord of all creation and that the created order is for him to use for his purposes. Those who know this and are his use the created order — food, drink, and human existence — for his purposes. *He* is central. His Lordship is central. We are central as we belong to *him* and try to live in accordance with his Spirit.

What we make of Jesus of Nazareth, therefore, is always in part determined by what we make of him for our lives now. If we think of him simply as a historical figure who lived two thousand years ago, we shall never understand him, for he was more than that. If, on the other hand, we consider his Spirit important for our lives now, but unrelated to the historical Jesus of Nazareth, we shall again miss him, for he was involved in a concrete historical situation and by his participation in it has given meaning to all history. In a word, Christian spirituality is rooted in the here and now as our own lives are led by the Spirit of Jesus of Nazareth, who was a particular unique person who lived at a particular time and in whom God did special things.

Any understanding of what God did in Christ two thousand years ago will help us understand what his Spirit is doing with us and in us here and now. The key to understanding is in our acknowledging and trusting that Spirit now. We can know that Spirit only as we are what we are — men of the twentieth century, living in the spirit of that century.

To turn to Jesus of Nazareth, then, in the spiritual life, we do not try to go back to find that historical figure and apply what we discover in that setting to our own historical situation. That procedure has a validity for a different approach and a different spirituality.

Rather, we proceed in just the opposite fashion — contemporary spirituality is entering fully into our own situation and trying to discover there the spirit which reveals the Lordship of Christ in *our* history. Our prayer is our reflection upon our history in the Spirit of him who is the Lord of all history and our response to that Spirit in the concrete historical events of our own day and our own lives.

What follows now are reflections upon some of the ordinary human experiences of a twentieth-century man in the light of the Spirit of Jesus of Nazareth. They are illustrations of contemporary spirituality, of a modern Christian style of life.

XII

ON GROWING UP

We begin not only with a world we never made but a life as well. We are thrust into the world through the decisions and acts of somebody else. How the world appears to us is determined largely by how our family appears to us. If we learn to trust our parents, we are helped to trust the world. If we are afraid of people, it is in some measure because we are afraid of our parents. God described to us as Father will raise up images either of a human father, who loves and cares for us, or of one who is a tyrant, whom we can never please.

Furthermore, we grow up as adults as we both accept and reject our parents. It is not either acceptance or rejection. It is both. Sometimes we only reject them. That is a loss, for they are part of us. Sometimes we only accept them, and that, too, is a loss, for we are meant to add something of our own.

This can be done as we assert ourselves because we believe we are somebodies in our own right. The reason for rejection so often is that only by rejection of our parents can we assert or find ourselves.

That scene of the boy, Jesus, in the Temple has always borne such an appeal because it describes such a universal situation — a child going off on his own, leaving his parents in search of something his parents have given him in part, but never wholly; going about his father's business, because only by doing so could he become himself. His parents do not make the self; they begin it. The self develops as he responds. That is growth. That is maturing. And that usually means pain.

> And when they saw him they were astonished; and his mother said to him, " Son, why have you treated us so? Behold, your father and I have been looking for you anxiously." And he said to them, " How is it that you sought me? Did you not know that I must be in my Father's house? " And they did not understand the saying which he spoke to them. And he went down with them and came to Nazareth, and was obedient to them; and his mother kept all these things in her heart.
> And Jesus increased in wisdom and in stature, and in favor with God and man.
>
> (Luke 2:48-52.)

We do not have to be literal-minded about the historical facts of this episode. We know that it is true, because the Spirit bears witness with our spirit in our own lives. It rings true to human experience.

We have to go about our father's business if we are ever to come to ourselves. Parents just simply do not understand at certain times. If a new person is to emerge from childhood, then the decision to reject a parent must be made in order to respond to the business his heavenly Father has in mind for him.

This is a spiritual matter. It can be stated this way: when a young person knows that if he is to come to his full self he must reject his family and does so, that is spiritual growth.

Granted all the ambiguities of self-will and mixed motivation, when all that has been cleared away and the time of decision to go or to stay has arrived, then the decision to go is a spiritual decision. Something new is being born. The self is striking out to find itself. The rightness is in the decision itself. It is spiritually sound because only so can the potential of the new self be realized. To remain at home is to remain a child. It is to dwell in the past, when what is called for is a new present.

One further comment: this spiritual growth is built into the

structure of life itself. This is not a Christian possession; it is
a human possession. Human beings cannot grow unless this
kind of spiritual growth takes place. To be sure, Christians
may be able to identify the experience in Christian terms that
have special meaning for them, such as leaving an earthly father to serve a heavenly Father. But the process is the same
for everyone who seeks human fulfillment and selfhood. This
is for them, as for Christians, their spiritual growth, indeed
their spiritual life.

The authority is in the action itself. It is immediately present. The rightness and the power are in the event. That is embedded in life itself. There does not have to be any reference
to a higher sanction or authority. It is self-authenticating. It *is*.

Its purpose, we may note, is the development of the human
life of the individual so that he might become an adult man,
a free and mature human being. The Spirit of Jesus of Nazareth, in other words, is always for man.

A further reflection follows directly upon this. It has to do
with forgiveness — mutual forgiveness, but, particularly here,
the forgiveness of parents by their children.

One of the wisest men of the twentieth century, Sigmund
Freud, once said, " Parents never die." We know this. We have
to come to terms with our parents sometime — either this side
of the grave or the other. This means accepting them.

The key to accepting them is to forgive them. We talk of
parents forgiving children, and that is quite proper at a certain age. But more profoundly in maturity, it is children growing to be able to forgive their parents.

Rebellion is a necessity in some instances if the self is to
be preserved. But after rebellion — what then? A broken relationship can be restored only by forgiveness. That's not so
easy. At least it is not when the pride of life and self-assur-
ance seem to be called for. Yet it is not possible to go about
our own destiny under God when we have repudiated those
who made our life and who are a part of us. That whole-
hearted dedication to one's own being rests upon an accept-

ance of one's parents. That means acceptance, forgiveness, and reconciliation.

Let us not be sentimental about the restoration of family relationships, but the fact is that Christ's life, death, and resurrection mean just exactly that — the restoration of everything broken into wholeness.

That Spirit-filled event in Christ means that, finally, the power of self-will is broken, and the power of love is permitted to heal all broken relationships. Everything is restored to wholeness. Brother is reconciled to brother, son to father, husband to wife, mother to daughter, man to God.

The Spirit of Jesus of Nazareth — the spiritual life — means forgiveness now. It means to live now — no more dwelling on old injuries and misunderstandings, no more hopes to settle scores in the future to gain sweet revenge. To live the spiritual life now is to forgive now — all who have hurt us — so that the reconciling love of God may heal and restore and make whole all relationships.

Reconciliation begins at home because that is where we started. By the power of the Spirit we can begin a new life in a new present. " Therefore, if any one is in Christ, he is a new creation; the old has passed away, behold, the new has come." (II Cor. 5:17.)

To put our own family situation into Christian perspective, let us turn again to Jesus of Nazareth and his family. Those " hidden years " in Nazareth formed for him, as our " hidden years " do for us, the background out of which he came to walk in his distinctive way with men. For him, as for us, there is the uniqueness of the family situation, which leads to the uniqueness each of us has as a mature adult.

He was, first of all, a nobody. That is, he was a nobody so far as his family was concerned because they weren't anybody. Later on, he was given a formidable genealogy (or genealogies), but when he was growing up he wasn't anybody because his family didn't count for anything.

To begin with, they lived in Galilee, and it was just natu-

rally assumed that nothing good could come out of that back-
ward rural area. He spoke Aramaic, the common speech of the
ordinary people. There is no evidence that he knew Greek or
was interested in Greek culture. As a rabbi acquainted with
the Scriptures as he was, he probably knew the Hebrew in
which they were written.

Although he was baptized by John the Baptist, he did not
follow the traditions of the rigorous ascetics and carry on his
ministry in the desert. Instead, he went into the villages and
small towns and later into the cities where the people were.
There he ate and drank with them. More important, he began
healing them and teaching that God's Kingdom was about to
begin.

He gathered disciples. He taught in the synagogue and in
the open air, always with a special air of authority as though
he had some inside knowledge. He took people, all kinds of
people — tax collectors, adulterers, fishermen, and children —
pretty much as they were and introduced them to the idea of
the Kingdom coming *right now*. He taught as a rabbi and
preached as a prophet. When he was accused of what we
would call a " role conflict," he appealed to no higher authority than himself. He refers to the Law, " You have heard that
it was said," and he goes on to comment, "but *I* say to
you . . ." (Matt. 5:21 f., 27 f., 31 f., 38 f., 43 f.). He taught them
" as one who had authority, and not as their scribes (Matt.
7:29). He drove out demons and healed the rich. His power
was immediate, made real right then and there. When people
met him, they knew they had met someone authentic. He made
the presence of God present!

As was to be expected, enemies eager to preserve the established order arose. In time, setting his face toward Jerusalem, he went to confront them. There he proclaimed once more
the coming of God's Kingdom, when God would be sovereign
over his created order. There he was put to death on the cross.

It was meant to be the end of Jesus of Nazareth. In reality,
it was the end of the all-sufficient world and of those who

considered themselves all-sufficient. From that time forth, God had to be reckoned with — for from now on he was to be present in the Spirit of Jesus, for whom the cross was not the ending but the beginning.

When we become aware of the Spirit, time crashes in. Each person is given a new present — still the same old world but no future in it. No longer can we rest on the past — our traditions go on, but they don't bear salvation. Only Jesus does. He brings it in each moment of time, for he is now the Lord — seen as the Lord by faith — and each person has that presence at each moment if he trusts him as Lord. We no longer have to dream of the future or put our hope in the future because the future is the Lord's. If we are his *now,* then we shall possess the future when he comes again.

The point is about the immediate authority of Jesus of Nazareth in the present. It is an absolute authority. It is his. It is exercised right now in this situation or that, in life as it is.

" ' Stretch out your hand.' He stretched it out, and his hand was restored." (Mark 3:5.) " And [he] said to him, . . . ' Be opened.' And his ears were opened, his tongue was released, and he spoke plainly." (Mark 7:34-35.) " And to the centurion Jesus said, ' Go; be it done for you as you have believed.' And the servant was healed at that very moment." (Matt. 8:13.)

The Spirit of Jesus of Nazareth breaks in on each " very moment " or life situation. Our spiritual life is determined by our response to that Spirit in that particular life situation. He is the Lord of that moment, of that situation. Our task is simply to acknowledge this and respond, then, through the circumstances of the situation, to *him.* That is the spiritual life.

The experience of the past obviously has some bearing on our response, but the present that comes with Jesus of Nazareth is always a new present. Therefore, we cannot be bound to old practices or traditions or principles. The key is response to the new Spirit that comes with each moment. We are to be bound to Jesus of Nazareth alone.

Nor can we be bound by undue concern for the future. We

cannot manipulate what will happen. The future is not ours. It belongs to Jesus of Nazareth. It was given him by the One God, his Father. Therefore, let not future hopes (or fears and anxieties, for that matter) decide what our response will be. The response can be in the Spirit of Jesus to him in the very moment that we have. That is the new present when Jesus comes again as Lord to make all things and us new.

The Spirit is in the circumstances of the situation, then. He is not to be found in principles of the past or in hopes of the future, but now. Our spiritual life is our decision, our action, our life as it is right now in response to him. Its character is forgiveness. It begins at home and goes on forever. It is a new life *now*.

XIII

ON AUTHORITY PROBLEMS

It has been said that all American males have, by the time they are forty, done something for which they should have been put in jail. American females apparently have a different set of values by which they live — not so obviously antisocial — but the principle is probably just as true for them.

"Thou shalt not cheat on examinations." That is the law. At least it is the law of school authority.

That law must somehow come to be written upon the inward heart — not simply obeyed. Until it is appropriated internally and becomes a part of oneself so that honor is lived, it always is broken — in spirit if not in fact.

Why shouldn't I cheat on examinations? There is no reason — unless I get caught — if that is the way to get ahead. Why shouldn't I get away with just as much as I can? I'll cut corners, fix scales, palm cards, load dice, keep an eye on the main chance, watch out for "No. 1" — because if I don't, nobody else will.

That's just plain natural. That's the way life is. That's human nature. That's what it is to be a man. That's to do what comes naturally.

It comes naturally to everybody. That's the trouble. Everybody else wants to be human, too, and to get what's coming to him, or what he thinks is coming to him. One man always thinks he deserves just a little bit more than the next fellow. So

he grabs for that little extra. So does everybody else. The result, of course, is chaos.

So the law. The law decides who gets what. The law determines what is right and just. One eye for one eye and one
tooth for one tooth — nothing could be fairer than that. Given
human nature — the hardness of our hearts — the law is a great
preserver of the peace.

It at least protects us from one another. If someone keeps
taking the spare tire out of my car trunk, I can appeal to the
law. Reuel Howe illustrates it in terms of a group of children
playing on the porch on a rainy day. Sooner or later a fight
breaks out as the children argue about who can use what toys.
That's where the law — carried by a parent — has to step in.
The parent lays the law down and says: " Stop it. You go there.
Give me that train engine. You come here. And the rest of you
behave or I'll send you all home." The law, says Howe, pre-
serves people — at least little people — from destroying themselves.

I won't obey the law, of course, if I can get away with it,
because the law interferes with my natural desires. It gets in
the way of my getting my way. Whether I obey it or not depends, then, upon the authority it has. Can the lawgiver en-
force the law? A young boy may obey the law and keep quiet
because the teacher clips him on the side of the head. Besides,
the teacher is bigger than he is.

But that authority is resented. Nobody likes to be told what
to do. I'll get back in some other way if I possibly can. I'll put
tacks in his seat, or draw pictures on the wall. Once school is
out and his authority is gone, I'll sing, " No more pencils. No
more books. No more teachers' nasty looks" — a spontaneous
and universal hymn of joy sung by generations of children at
last set free to return to nature.

In the psychological language of the day, I have an authority problem. Most everybody has an authority problem. It is
nothing to be ashamed of. It's a natural human thing to have.
In some way, I shall have to — as they say — " work it through."

Maybe I can do it by hitting a golf ball or knocking out flies. If I find I hit my wife and children or become surly to my colleagues at work, that's a good sign I'd better work it through by talking to a psychiatrist. Let me take out my hostilities on him. That's in part what he gets paid for.

To sum up: there is the law; there is the lawgiver; there is the authority; and then my rebellion and resentment of the authority figure.

But what if the lawgiver likes me? Suppose the authority figure becomes more important to me than the law? What if the law turns out simply to be the way to discover that there is, in fact, a lawgiver? What happens if I should see that my behavior is not nearly so important as my trust? What happens when I discover that the law is given so that I might learn what the lawgiver is like? that the main thing about him is that he likes me? even loves me?

The young Turkish student mentioned in one of the letters finally became trustworthy because he was trusted by somebody who could clip him on the ear, but who beyond that (the boy knew) liked him, maybe even loved him. The honor system was only a bridge to honor. It got across through a personal relationship expressed through law, but it represented a good deal more than law. What was crucial was not the values — either obedience to the external law or to inner integrity — but the personal relationship of trust.

So, then, consider these words of Jesus:

> You have heard that it was said, " You shall love your neighbor and hate your enemy." But I say unto you, Love your enemies and pray for those who persecute you, so that you may be sons of your Father who is in heaven; for he makes his sun rise on the evil and on the good, and sends rain on the just and on the unjust. For if you love those who love you, what reward have you? Do not even the tax collectors do the same? And if you salute only your brethren, what more are you doing than others? Do not even the Gentiles do the same? You, therefore, must be perfect, as your heavenly Father is perfect.
>
> (Matt. 5:43-48.)

What he appears to be saying on one level is, Don't think you can justify yourself by meeting the law. You can't. The law gets tighter and tighter. You can't ever begin on human ground and pick up a ladder of behavior and begin to climb higher and higher, thinking each step up — no more sex, no more drinks, no more cigarettes, more prayers, more confessions, more Sacraments — brings you closer to God. No. You will never, never make it. You will get toppled sooner or later, if for no other reason than you say to yourself one day, " See how high I am." Then pride strikes the ladder down, and you begin all over again.

On a deeper level, however, Jesus is doing what he always is doing — pointing to God. We are meant to be sons of our Father; let us turn, therefore, to him. We have to be perfect as he is perfect. Keep our eyes, therefore, on him.

" Repent, for the kingdom of heaven is at hand." (Matt. 4:17.) Turn back from our old ways of self-will, for something new is about to happen — God's Kingdom is right here. The earlier Gospel puts the message of Jesus in this way: " Now after John was arrested, Jesus came into Galilee, preaching the gospel of God, and saying, ' The time is fulfilled, and the kingdom of God is at hand; repent, and believe in the gospel ' " (Mark 1:14). That is his message. Right at the beginning, that is his message.

God is in control. We may not see it with our natural eyes, but his control is exercised right now in all the ways of the world. If we had the eyes of faith, we would see it. We must see what is about to happen. There it is, hidden in the seed being sown, in the leaven raising bread, in the coin found, the son returned, the children dancing, the blind man healed. Don't you see what is happening? Don't try to force its coming; leave the tares and wheat together until the time comes; it's not ours to attain and possess; it is God's to give. We have only to repent and believe. Then we have hope. So trust him. Repent and believe.

The history of Israel illustrates this. The law is the sign of that covenant relationship established by God with his chosen people. The relationship of being chosen is more important than the codes of behavior. God and Israel are the parties to the covenant. God has selected Israel to be his people. For Israel, the relationship is one of trust, dependence, thanksgiving, and, *therefore,* obedience. The modern man, emancipated from his religious tradition, who says it is more important to be good than to believe in God, has lost that distinctive Biblical note of personal trust in a Creator who loves, suffers, pleads, dies. A principle of morality displaces a person. Something vital is lost. The law has come back again.

Jesus said that if you put your trust in your ability to obey the law, you have built an obstacle between yourselves and God. What was meant to be a bridge has become a barrier. The law was given to bring you to God, and you have turned it to protect yourself from him. Your self-righteousness becomes your defense. When it does, God strikes it down.

We are not, in other words, to put our trust in the law, but in the lawgiver, not in our obedience to rules of behavior, but in him who loves us despite our behavior.

There are certain questions that press for answers. One is: Do our human values reflect divine values? There is another level that asks the same question: Is there any truth that exists apart from our truth — or our understanding of it — and is yet related to it? Or, again on a third level: Does it make any difference — any *real* difference — how we behave? Who cares?

Ask these questions of Jesus of Nazareth and he answers — as always — by pointing to God. You are meant, he says, to live as his sons — right now. Therefore, repent, trust, and obey. The law is not destroyed; it is fulfilled. It is fulfilled, however, not by an additional " law," more rigorous demands laid upon men. It is fulfilled by him whose law it is, because it is his Kingdom. That Kingdom is to be ushered in immediately.

Therefore, God is present right now, if we only have faith to believe it. All we need do is trust and obey him. Look, there is his Kingdom in the work you do and the wages you receive; in the wife you kiss and the child you spank; in the dance hall and bar; on the picket line and in those riots. Don't you see? God is there in all the human joy and anguish. " He who has ears, let him hear." (Matt. 13:43.)

This does not resolve the tension or conflict between our life on earth and God's will for our life on earth. It does make it bearable. More than that, however, it brings a whole new perspective, a new present, a new self, a new loyalty, a new truth, a new affirmation: God reigns!

Of course, there is judgment. But in and through the judgment there is hope. God's Kingdom is now. So we live directly related to God now; must make our decisions in relation to him now; must live in terms of our human situation now, because this is where God's Kingdom is. Therefore, there is no end to the new possibilities of that situation. They are not what the world sees. They are what God commands. We are only to trust and obey. He is at hand.

If we take seriously, then, the question of human values, Jesus of Nazareth points us to God. If we ask him questions about truth apart from our experience of truth, he points us to God. If we ask who cares, he points us to God.

He doesn't directly answer with words any of our questions. He bears in himself, however, the word, the answer, to all our questions. " Be sons of your Father who is in heaven " — trust him, obey him — then you will find your answers.

So the answers come to those who are sons in exactly reverse order: (1) God cares. (2) His truth is his will and exists independent of our knowledge of it; you know it only as you obey it. (3) Yes, there is a reflection of divine values in human values, of divine law in human law, for the law points to God.

The answer is, God cares. But he doesn't care so much about our behavior as he cares about *us*. Or, he cares about our behavior *because* he cares about us. If all we do is try to behave better and better so that he will begin to care, we get it all wrong. He already cares. That is shown in Christ. Once we see that our failures to meet the requirements of the law lead us to God, then we can open our eyes to begin to see what Christ is like, and that starts to get it all right. " The law," says Paul, " was our custodian until Christ came, that we might be justified by faith. But now that faith has come, we are no longer under a custodian; for in Christ Jesus you are all sons of God, through faith." (Gal. 3:24-26.)

We see, then, the tension between God's will and our behavior, but beyond that as we see *him*, we can honestly hunger and thirst after righteousness. It is in response to him and for his sake, because of our trust in him and not because we are trying to make our peace with him or to impress him, that we have that hunger. That makes all the difference in the world. That makes it bearable.

XIV

ON LOVE LETTERS FOR MONKS

Why a love letter read to monks?

There are three reasons. The first one is, why not?

Love is a perfectly natural human experience. It comes to all kinds of men and women under all kinds of circumstances. Many men who are now monks — and women who are sisters — have had this experience. They have simply at some time said no to a person's love for the sake of the love of God. That is their free human choice. It may make them more human than any other choice. At least it is their free decision. But that has not made them exempt from the human experience of love, for they are, with the rest of us, part and parcel of common humanity — and that is shot through with love.

The second is a reminder: human love is the bearer of God's love. Let us not put human love on one side and God's love on another. Let us not make *eros* and *agape* a Janus-like love with two faces looking in opposite directions.

Now, to be sure, there is a difference. There is a love that demands and seeks to possess, and there is a love that is the expression of concern for another and does not seek to possess. To be sure, man is not God, and his ways are not our ways. There is a distinction between human love and divine love.

But divine love does not cancel out human love. Indeed, it is in and through the human relationships that divine relationships are known. *Agape* — God's pure love — is expressed in and through human relationships, twisted and distorted by human twisting and distortion, but *there* nonetheless. If *agape* is not known there, where, indeed, is it known?

Derrick Sherwin Bailey defines love as a personal relationship where a man and a woman meet and know one another; they also meet and know themselves; and in that meeting and knowing they come to meet and know God.

To put it another way: when a man and a woman are in love, they commit themselves to one another in trust, in what has come to be called an I-thou relationship. This means that the knowledge you have of another person comes in the " inside " way where you say " you " to a person and the other person says " you " in response.

It is always second person singular. When I say to my wife, " I love *you*," this is quite different from saying, " I love my wife." She has become a third person singular, an " it " rather than a " you." When I try to describe her, saying " she " is so tall, looks like this, acts like that, I haven't described her at all; I have told about some externals. What she is — when I really know her — is when I say " you." Personal knowledge, then, is always inside knowledge that comes when love and trust make possible an I-thou relationship. In the same way, she has knowledge of me (poor soul!) that nobody else has, because it is personal and rests upon her saying " you " in love and trust.

The eternal " thou " who is speaking through all such human loves is God. Through a human relationship of love he is calling his loved ones to know that he is one who loves them. The eternal *fact* of his love exists for all men; the *experience* of that love is carried in and through human love. So it may be said not simply that a man and a woman in love point to God's love; they are the bearers of God's love to one another.

The emphasis is again upon the immediacy of God's Kingdom. Where are its signs? Where is his love? All about us — right in the stuff of life, right where we are now, right in the midst of our human situation.

For most people, their most personal human situation is where they are in love. Though they may not know it, that is where God is.

Of course, this love is not pure and undefiled. Who said it was supposed to be? There is always in human love a yearning for possession — to know one another physically. This is part of what it is to be a man. But does not God yearn for man's love? Is his love not to be compared to the love that a man has for his wife — even his faithless wife? There is sound Biblical authority for saying so.

So it is, then, in all personal love relationships — of which the most personal is marriage — that the meeting and the knowing of man and God goes on. It is in and through these relationships that God has his most personal dealings with man. Therefore, a love letter is as sound a devotional reading for monks as for pagans.

Indeed, this is one way by which pagans can come to understand the nature of the Gospel, for if they love, if they respond, if they argue and separate, if they forgive one another, if they come together again, they are in touch not simply with one another but with God.

Our problem is not so much that we have tried to make man too spiritual, although that is probably true. More important, we have not made God human enough. When we spiritualize our love by removing it from man and giving it to God, we run the risk of becoming dehumanized, too spiritual, too desiccated, and we dry up. If God is considered as the source, the well from which all human love springs, then those human relationships maintain their freshness and vigor, their exhilaration and their beauty.

When we speak of human love, we cannot speak of it as though it were only human. God's love is always mixed up — terribly mixed up — with it. When love comes, God comes.

Love always comes, for example, as a gift. People don't make it up. They don't say, "let us go now and we shall fall in love."

No, it comes. "One day," they say, "it came to us that we were in love. It happened to us — not we happened to it."

When it comes, it judges us. The young man always says, "I wish I were worthy of her love." He regrets what he has done and what he has been.

Beyond that, however, love makes us over — never completely but in some measure. "She sees in me," he says, "something nobody else has ever seen, but I've suspected it was there all along. She draws it out of me." He becomes more of a person than he was.

It isn't necessary to spell out the analogy. The gospel comes always as a gift; we do not deserve it, nor is it of our own making. When it comes, it judges us; we are convicted because we know in its light that there is no health in us. But it also redeems us, strengthens us, gives us new power and strength for living.

He who has eyes to see, let him see. This is what is going on. God is in touch with a man and a woman in love, telling them of his love.

That love is expressed in a variety of ways in every human situation of which they are a part. There are three ways in particular, though love is a total mixture, and it is impossible to separate them into neat divisions.

There is first that yearning, that longing to know and possess which promises fulfillment, wholeness, completion, release. This is *eros,* the love that demands for oneself. Its roots are deeper than sexual but include sex. Sexuality is more than sex, for it expresses a whole personality.

Sexual love is no more to be thought of as evil than is physical hunger. As a part of the created order, it is good, as it is God's. It may be corrupted, of course (the corruption, however, is in man's self-will — not in sex), but in itself it is a human drive that helps make man what he is.

A bishop was once responsible for a position being offered to a priest. After a long consideration, it seemed to the priest that, while there was nothing wrong with it, it just wasn't for him. He reported this reaction to the bishop, who replied, "Well, it's like marriage. There is no point in getting married to a girl if you don't want to go to bed with her, is there?" Precisely.

Along with *eros* there is *philia* — simple friendship. It's good for wives and husbands to like each other, though it doesn't always happen. When friendship is added to erotic love, the ties are so much the stronger. A friend once commented, "Much to my surprise, my wife has turned out to be my best friend." Happy surprise!

The third side, of course, is *agape* — the outgoing selfless concern for another, that love which does not try to get its own way but wants only what is best for one's beloved. This is God's love for man. But it is in man's love for man as well, for it is human love at its best. The great thing about love is that for once we are concerned not about ourselves but another. We love another just as much as we love ourselves — for another self has become part of our self.

There are just two further words to be said. One is that when a man and a woman are in love they are euphoric. That is, they have a sense of well-being that colors their entire outlook on life. They know that they belong to one another and, therefore, that they are safe. They belong to the world. They are safe in their love for each other and, therefore, need not be ashamed to acknowledge their love for themselves.

In psychological terms, they are given ego strength. They can affirm the self, their own self. This strength is different from a self-assertive, ruthless strength that dominates and is proud of itself. It is, rather, a quiet acceptance of the self as worthy and, therefore, there is no need to be afraid or even guilty.

From this point of view, it is not possible to think too highly of oneself. One is loved. Therefore, one is complete and fulfilled. One belongs. One simply *is* and is content to be. He does not have to strive to prove anything. He knows, even as he is known.

The second word is that the knowing, of course, finally is the knowing by God, the loving by God. He is the one who keeps coming through the relationships — always to love, always to express concern, always to do what is for our good.

He comes in judgment, demanding obedience, and that is how we come to our fullest selves, our most complete selves, our true selves. It is always in these love relationships, this belonging to one another, meeting and knowing one another, that love is expressed.

Lest this give too idyllic a picture of love and marriage, let me say simply that this is a package deal. It all comes together: the sickness and the health, the wealth and the poverty, the love and the hostility, the pain and the joy, the temptations and the faithlessness, the victories and the failures.

So we are not talking about paradise. We are talking about life on earth, human life and a marriage made up of two self-willed, opinionated people. *Agape* helps. *Agape* puts you in the place of the other one. *Agape* takes you out of your self. But it's never pure *agape*: husbands come home late for supper and wives don't get shirts clean on time. Adultery in spirit if not in the flesh is never far from the surface. Faithlessness and boredom may become the marks of the marriage rather than love, trust, and joy. The man and woman brought together out of their separate wells of loneliness into a mutual union all too often after the first argument find themselves falling back into their separate isolations.

When this happens, the only way separation is overcome is by one person saying, "I'm sorry. Let's start over again." That is, someone is willing to die a little to pride and self-will and getting one's own way for the sake of the other, for his own sake — even for God's sake.

This dying to self — this little cross — is in one way or another embedded deeply in every human marriage. It is what makes it divine. Love is held together, finally, by just this patient willingness to accept each other, to forgive each other, and to begin again. It is not often dramatic, but it is the stuff of life in many homes.

Love, then, can bear all kinds of hostilities and survive — even become stronger. When one husband came home late for supper for the hundredth time to the increasing annoyance of his wife, she finally confronted him, " What am I supposed to be getting out of this marriage, anyway? " He replied, " You are getting a fellow human being whom you can get mad at — just as mad as you want to — and who still loves you, no matter what."

That's quite a gift. It comes only in love. Love bears — indeed, sometimes expresses — hostility. In any case, only in love can you express hostility properly.

There is one last word: in the state of matrimony there is represented " the spiritual marriage and unity betwixt Christ and his Church." This point is made by (of all people) Paul, who was unenthusiastic enough about marriage to commend it only as preferable to burning. He is talking in Ephesians (that is, if he wrote it) about the relationship of husband and wife and the relationship of Christ and his church. " Be subject," he says, " to one another out of reverence for Christ. Wives, be subject to your husbands, as to the Lord. For the husband is the head of the wife as Christ is the head of the church, his body, and is himself its Savior. As the church is subject to Christ, so let wives also be subject in everything to their husbands. Husbands, love your wives, as Christ loved the church and gave himself up for her." (Eph. 5:21-25.) Then he concludes: " ' For this reason a man shall leave his father and mother and be joined to his wife, and the two shall become one.' This is a great mystery, and I take it to mean Christ and the church." (Eph. 5:31-32.)

Marriage is where most people can come to understand what the church is. It is giving and receiving; it is judging and being judged; it is forgiving and being forgiven; it is trusting and being trusted; it is accepting and being accepted; it is loving and being loved; it is being in union and yet becoming more of a person; it is dying to self and living a resurrected life; it is wanting not to have your own way and finding self-fulfillment in self-emptying; it is bearing a cross together and so being bound ever closer to one another.

What human beings experience from time to time in the life of their marriage is, in fact, what the life of the church is. Love is not always experienced as such among the members of the church, but there can be no doubt that that is its essential nature because Christ is its head.

The key is: to whom is the response? If the response is to Christ — through the church to Christ — then there is established and set forth the I-thou relationship with him who is our head. It is then that we have the most intimate dealings with another. It is then that we know who we are and who Christ is and what he wants us to do — or what we want to do — as an expression of our love.

We miss this if our response is to anything less than Christ and stops there. We miss it if we respond only, for example, to the institutional church, or to institutions within the church, or to budgets, or to desires to succeed, or to fears of failure. It is not that there is anything wrong with any of these parts of the body. The body is human as well as divine. But they are all " its." Our response is to a " thou " — you, Christ, who are our head.

So we respond in and through all the structures set around us — but none of the structures is Christ. He is in and around and through them. But he cannot be identified with any one of them.

It's like marriage. It's worked out in budgets and in bed and in eating and raising a family and going on picnics and paying bills and having arguments and getting mad and saying, " I'm sorry," and in loving and trusting each other and having good times together. The response is always a personal one to each in an I-thou relationship.

That's what membership in the family of Christ is like. The response finally is always to him in an I-thou relationship between the members and the Head.

XV

ON SAYING YES

The most remarkable spiritual autobiography of our day is *Markings*, by Dag Hammarskjöld. He describes it as "'a kind of white paper' concerning my negotiations with myself and God."

Our negotiations with ourselves and God are prayer. They can be called by any number of terms — reflections, broodings, conversations, thoughts. They reflect a very natural human enterprise on which all men at some time or another are engaged. Indeed, such negotiations lead to the decisions we make and result in actions.

We often, if we want further wisdom than our own, negotiate with others. What do they think? What has been their experience? What is their opinion about what will happen if such and such an action is taken? We talk with our contemporaries or read what they have written. Through the written record, we negotiate with the minds of men long dead. This method of entering into the mind and spirit of others is the way by which we come to a decision. In that decision we reveal what we think the right action is, and in that action we reveal ourselves.

When the negotiations involve oneself and others, that is one thing. When the negotiations involve God, however, that is something else again. Something new enters in. Then our response is not simply to others but also to him. That is prayer. Dag Hammarskjöld put it this way in an entry dated Whitsunday, 1961:

> I don't know Who — or what — put the question. I don't know when it was put. I don't even remember answering. But at some moment I did answer Yes to Someone — or Something — and from that hour I was certain that existence is meaningful and that, therefore, my life, in self-surrender, had a goal.[1]

That marks the line as clearly as it can be marked. The response now is to God. Response to man is included. Nothing that belongs to man is excluded. But beyond the human there is another dimension. When life is lived within that dimension, then the continuing negotiations are with God as well as with men. That is the spiritual life. " In our era," Hammarskjöld remarks, " the road to holiness passes through the world of action." [2]

Another way of putting it is to say that when we respond to God we are responding to him who has the final control of life, in whom " the last things " are brought to completion. We are, however, given control over " the immediate things " of this world. They are " next to last." It is only through the things of this world — the day-by-day things, our secular actions in a secular world — that it is possible to respond to God. We cannot escape from this world — we are not meant to — but we are turned back into it. Therefore, matters " spiritual " are jobs and housing and civil rights and equal educational opportunities and casting votes intelligently. In a word, the spiritual life is the involved life — involved with those immediate things of this world.

There are, of course, countless ways of involvement, intel-

---

[1] Dag Hammarskjöld, *Markings* (Alfred A. Knopf, Inc., 1964), p. 205.

[2] *Ibid.*, p. 122.

lectual as well as physical, national as well as international, with the prosperous in suburbia as with the poor in the city. The point is that we do not go it alone. The Christian man is the man who belongs to his society and works through the social structures as well as through personal relationships to make his faith clear.

Therefore, we don't have to be unduly concerned about what happens. If our response is to God on the basis of what we understand him to be, then the results will have to be his. In a sense, the results don't matter if the reason for a decision is to make it in response to God.

What is important, in other words, is the source of the action rather than the results. It simply means acting in accordance with the Spirit of God as we know it at the time; it is acting from the welling up of our deepest inner convictions, out of the ground of our being.

When the Spirit of Christ was given at Pentecost, that was all that was given. Peter could not explain anything on that day except that the gift of the Spirit was associated with Jesus of Nazareth, who was crucified and raised from the dead. The mark of the Christians was that they then acted in response to that Spirit. They did not know what the actions would lead to. They were not particularly concerned with results. That was God's business. Their business was to respond to the Spirit. Period.

Another way of saying this is to affirm the existential character of life. *Now* is the time. There is no other. We must live; let us live. Past time and future time bear in upon the present time, to be sure, but the only time in which we may act is this time now.

Jesus of Nazareth was very impatient with those who questioned him about what was going to happen.

> Being asked by the Pharisees when the kingdom of God was coming, he answered them, " The kingdom of God is not coming with signs to be observed; nor will

they say, 'Lo, here it is!' or 'There!' for behold, the kingdom of God is in the midst of you."

And he said to the disciples, "The days are coming
when you will desire to see one of the days of the Son of
man, and you will not see it. And they will say to you,
'Lo, there!' or 'Lo, here!' Do not go, do not follow
them. For as the lightning flashes and lights up the sky
from one side to the other, so will the Son of man be in
his day."

(Luke 17:20-25.)

No, he said, salvation is right here and now because it is
God's and his Kingdom has come. Belong to it. Trust it. Let
God worry about the rest. You do not know when the end of
all things will come. Now is the only time you have.

The terrible necessity for a decision right now is one
of the hard sayings of Jesus. Yet do not the existentialists the
same? The difference is that the Christian existentialist is
responding to God. In God is his trust. God puts new meaning
into the event.

Jesus apparently, for example, did not concern himself with
the political and national aspirations of his people as they
were expressed in the Jewish concept of the Messiah. He took
them as he found them and changed them. The very inscrip-
tion on the cross, "King of the Jews," became something
quite different from what the Jews or the Romans considered
it to be. Something new broke into the event and, therefore,
into the meaning of the title.

Don't try to know too much, he says. Don't look for signs.
Don't try to assure the future. The Kingdom is God's — not
yours. The future is his — not yours. What you are called to
is action now, just where you are. Do this and the future —
God's future — is then opened to you.

We do not, therefore, have to ask, where are the signs?
God has already provided the signs in the mighty acts recorded in the Biblical story and in the movement of the
gospel right through history. To ask for special "proofs" —

such as, prayer "works," faith "heals," families that "pray together stay together" — is to fall into the perfect trap of worldliness.

No, says Jesus of Nazareth, don't try to get signs. Put your trust in God. Repent, trust, obey. Go about your worldly business; concentrate on those next to last things which are yours to work with. Where else do you think I am?

That brings us to the final point. It is put this way by Hammarskjöld: "At some moment I did answer *Yes* . . . and from that hour I was certain that existence is meaningful and that, therefore, my life, in self-surrender, had a goal." [3]

In other words, the truth about life — existential, living truth — comes through trust and obedience. When we *do* the truth, we know it. It comes to us. It reveals itself to us. It communicates itself to us.

The problem is so often presented to us in philosophical language dealing with immense concepts that are difficult for us to grasp. For example, "What is truth?" is such an enormous question that we throw up our hands in despair. Jesus refused to answer this question when Pilate asked him and in general refused to get into philosophical disputations with the Pharisees and others. They wanted signs and proofs. He said: That is not the way God is known. He is known through judgment and salvation now.

The fact is, of course, that the answer is revealed bit by bit in little, ordinary human ways, often hidden from sight at the time. "What shall I do with my life?" is too big a question for most of us to answer. But we have to answer yes to this person or that person, to this job or to that job, if we are to eat.

We don't have to worry about the long-term purpose of our vocation, or the vocations of the institutions for which we may be responsible; we have to decide whether we shall trust and obey God in the immediate situation where we are.

[3] *Ibid.*, p. 205.

We don't have to know very much about either God or ourselves. The negotiations simply call for our giving what we do know about ourselves to what we know about God. If we do that — if we say *yes* — then we shall discover that our existence is meaningful and our life has a goal.

XVI

ON ACCEPTING AND CHANGING

Nature is, of course, both good and evil, or, more accurately, it is neutral, and whether it is good or evil depends upon your point of view.

During the Second World War, a Navy ship went through three typhoons. One of them destroyed every small boat in Buckner Bay in Okinawa and many not so small. The men on that ship obviously did not have a very high regard for typhoons. Yet the navigator commented one day that the same typhoons which cause so much destruction in the South Pacific each year also water the coast of China and prevent it from turning into a desert. So the Chinese welcome the same storms the Okinawans curse.

The rain falls on the just and the unjust alike. The sun rises on the evil and the good. The fowl of the air build their nests and fly hither and yon. The lilies of the field grow and flourish; the fig trees put out leaves each spring. There is a regular cycle of the seasons. Flowers rise up; weeds get tangled with them; they finally wither and die.

You can't infer God from nature. Because there is an order in nature — a neutral order, neither good nor evil — it does not follow that there is God.

It is the other way around. For Jesus of Nazareth it was always the other way around. God begins and sustains the world of nature. He thought it up; he is behind every continuing act of creation. If we begin with him, then we can see how nature speaks of him and his work. See, not a sparrow falls without his knowledge. So are the hairs of our heads counted. He takes care of the birds, doesn't he? Why, then, are we so anxious? We are of more value than they.

Once we assume God as creator, the responsible one behind all that is created, then everything in nature, including human nature, points beyond itself to God. Once we begin with God and then look at life, we see with the eyes of faith things going on that we did not see with our natural eyes.

Jesus of Nazareth simply assumed the God of the Old Testament, who is the creator who cares for his creation as he governs it. All nature, therefore, may speak of him; may be a parable that provides the earthly story with a heavenly meaning; may be the means by which he touches man. The universe itself is sacramental — the outward and visible reflecting, bearing the inner and spiritual. It always points to more than it is itself; it points to God.

What this means, then, is that we take life as it comes. There is an order in nature that we are not going to overcome. So we'd better take it just as it is. If we are on a ship when the typhoons come, we'd better make the best of it and do our best to survive; and if we are on the coast of China, we can give thanks. In each instance, God is still in control. He still cares. He will resolve all issues finally. Therefore, trust him.

To say that we are to take life as it comes does not mean to accept it passively and not try to do anything about it. When floods come, we'd better control them; when droughts come, we'd better have irrigation trenches dug; when lightning strikes, we put out the fire.

Man is meant to be responsible and to control nature for his good. He puts his labor to work and adds something by the sweat of his brow. We can't, however, find our whole meaning of life in that which we create. We store everything we accumulate in barns, and then one night we die — and then where are we? That relationship with God beyond nature and beyond what we do with nature is the key relationship.

It has to do with human nature. How do we accept our own nature when we get so sick of it? We begin by accepting it.

Michel Quoist puts it bluntly:

> As long as you refuse to accept yourself as you are, you will never be able to build a full life for yourself because you will spend all your time wishing you had the tools that others have to build their lives without recognizing what you already have at your disposal. Your tools may be different but they can be just as good for your purposes. . . .
>
> If there is something you can change, what are you waiting for? Get busy, but with a calm perseverance. If there is something you can't change, accept it as it is. It's not a matter of " resigning " yourself to your fate by hanging your head in despair. You have to learn to lift it up and say yes to reality. It's not a matter of letting yourself be bested by it. Bear it and offer it to God. . . .
>
> Accept yourself, but accept yourself in relation to others. . . . If you are afraid of others, remember that you will only begin to make a favourable impression on them if you accept yourself as you are, for you can never be the other, and in developing your own personality you provide a complement to the personalities of others.
>
> Don't seek to live somebody else's life; it's just not you. The Father has given each of us a life to live. . . .
>
> Be yourself. Others need you just as the Lord has willed you to be.[1]

We do much the same with our social order. We have to take this as it comes, also, and then change what can be changed. Jesus never said very much about the separation of church and state, or the best forms of government for the establishment of justice and peace, or what political theory best understood the nature of man. He naturally accepted a social structure as part of the way things were. " Give Caesar,"

[1] Michel Quoist, *The Christian Response* (Dublin: M. H. Gill & Sons, Ltd., 1963), pp. 50–53.

he says, "the things that are Caesar's." Pay taxes. Do your
military service. Fight wars if necessary. All this is part and
parcel of the stuff of life, and you take it as it comes. But,
more important than that, "give to God the things that are
God's." *You* are God's and you have to give yourself to him.
You can do it as a member of an earthly kingdom because
you know that – more important – you are a member of
God's Kingdom.

We can hear Jesus' point of view: don't just acquiesce in
what society is or the government wants. You have a responsibility to make it a more just society, more free of injustice
and segregation and poverty and ignorance. Work as hard
as you can on these things. Just remember, however, you are
God's. Your salvation does not depend on them – on your
doing them – but on God.

Since we are citizens of the state, we have the responsibility
to try to have that state conform to the best ideals of mankind. We use our best judgment as to how to do this. It
may be in picket lines, in civil disobedience, in strikes. Or it
may be we find we can do it best by working patiently within
the structures set by the state. This is the reason for different
parties and philosophies and ideologies. There is meant to
be a struggle for power in which men are involved that a
more just social order may emerge. Just remember, in all
this we are God's. Our trust is meant to be in him, not in any
political or social structure of our own making.

Of course, the heart of man is evil. Yet there is always this
goodness embedded in it, never quite extinguished, and at
times bursting forth in great acts of courage and heroism. The
goodness of men aboard a ship is one thing, but the troops
who board her are the enemy. I'm out to protect my own.

So, of course, we don't put our trust in man. We put it in
God. We are his, aren't we?

So we use our judgment, as intelligently as we can, to create
structures of control nationally and internationally. These
structures of this world are important to build and to refine

that there may be greater areas of justice and opportunities for peace. But they are not all-important, for they belong to Caesar. We belong to Caesar now, but we also belong to God — now and forever.

Yet while we are here, we belong to each other. We cannot worship God in the abstract or trust him by withdrawing from life. He calls us to trust him through our neighbor; he calls us through the needs of our neighbor to meet those needs. That is to love him, to go about meeting his needs.

Who is our neighbor? Who is our buddy? Well, he is not only our shipmate; he is the soldier who comes along for the ride as a passenger; he is our enemy. He is the one who needs *us*. Never mind the reasons why we cannot pause to help — previous commitments, religious duties. No, says Jesus of Nazareth, cut through all that right to the heart of the need of the other man. Put yourself in his place. See his need? Well, then, how are you going to go about helping him? How are you going to love him as you love yourself? You in your neighbor — how are you going to love yourself *there?*

XVII

ON THE SUCCESS OF FAILURE

Success and failure are part and parcel of life. *Good thoughts for bad times* have their counterpart — *bad thoughts for good times.* If every cloud has a silver lining it is no less true that there is a dark side to life. Happy is he whose failures go with his successes!

It is one thing to accept the goodness of life — happy times, work to do, friends and people who love you. In a sense, the best things in life *are* free. But in another sense, the best things in life cost dearly. Perhaps the costliness lies closer to the heart of life than the happiness. Or, it may be in that curious intermingling of joy and pain that we find the secret of the mystery of what it truly is to be a man — at least a man under God.

The fact of suffering surely doesn't have to be pressed home today. We see those pictures from Vietnam: a mother holding a child whose head is bleeding, a young boy sitting by his mother's body covered with a blanket, a father pushing his parents in a wheelbarrow. No matter how many assurances are given that only a few civilians were hit, we know that war is hell and brings inevitably untold suffering among the innocent citizens as well as the professional soldiers.

Suffering hits home hardest, of course, when it's personal. It's hard for me to know anything about toothaches until it is my tooth that aches. Then my whole head throbs, and I say to myself, "Nobody ever had such a toothache as I have."

After an automobile accident, a friend was in a hospital for six weeks with a head injury of such a nature that medication could not be given. When it was all over, she commented: "If anybody had asked me my name then, I would have said, 'My name is pain.' I was nothing but pain — a throbbing being. Nobody can ever know what it is like." Pain separates a person from everybody else.

It doesn't have to be dramatic. Gossip separates people, too. What is it about men and women that causes them to tell stories about others, to belittle them, we say? I suppose it is because this way we build ourselves up higher or think we do. But gossip betrays people, it breaks down trust, it separates them from each other. When we speak about a person behind his back, we make it impossible to talk to him face to face, which is the only way we can come to trust each other.

Ezra Pound asks: "When one's friends hate each other, how can there be peace in the world?"

This, strangely enough, is true even of friends who are friends of God. The psalms raised this question again and again.

> It is not an enemy who taunts me —
> then I could bear it;
> it is not an adversary who deals in-
> solently with me —
> then I could hide from him.
> But it is you, my equal,
> my companion, my familiar friend.
> We used to hold sweet converse together;
> within God's house we walked in
> fellowship.
>
> (Ps. 55:12–15.)

You may know of one clergyman's comment after he had engaged a curate: "Remember, now, that there is only one thing worse than being a curate, and that is having one."

Why is it that one of the perennial problems in the ministry is the difficulty clergy have in getting along with each other?

Despite the current vogue of team ministries, I know of just one that has lasted for more than eight years. What is it that separates us like this?

Well, one could go on at length about the experiences of life that isolate us. Self-will. I want my way. You want your way, so we have a tug of war. Do you remember the figure Søren Kierkegaard used when he described life as meant to be a circle, with people joining hands together around God, who is in the center? Each person, however, keeps putting himself in the center. The result is confusion, everybody tangled up and separated from everyone else.

The final separation, of course, is death. When someone dies, then he is separated forever. He is gone — as they say in hospitals — " out."

So much for one observable fact of human life: failure, gossip, suffering, pain, self-will, sin, death — all have in common the power of separating men from men.

Now another fact, not quite so obvious: the really powerful people are those who have suffered. At least there seems to be a relationship of some kind between pain and power. The more pain, the more of a man.

A philosopher (Illingworth) has put it like this: " The men of sorrows are the men of influence. Even more than knowledge pain is power." A poet (Wordsworth) has put it this way: " A deep distress hath humanized my soul." It is pain that makes a man a man.

We can test it best by simply asking, "When we need help most, who gives it to us best? " It is not the successful ones, the ones who have always had smooth going, to whom we turn, is it? Don't we instinctively turn to those who have themselves been in trouble and suffered? Maybe we turn to them and talk to them. More probably we just turn and watch them or simply remember them. Or perhaps somebody just tells us about them. That, somehow, is enough: some strength comes from them to us in some hidden way.

Early in my ministry I saw a good deal of a retired professor whose wife was dying of cancer. After her death, he went off on a fishing trip with an old crony of his. Ten days later he was stricken with multiple sclerosis and was back in bed in the same room where his wife had been ill for so long.

I asked him one day what sense he made of this, and he replied: "Well, I've been through this once before. During the influenza epidemic after the First World War, my first wife and one of our three children died. I went away then to try to figure out why this should happen to me. You know, I never did figure it out, but I learned that life was spelling out for me a four-letter word, d-u-t-y. So I came back home, and ever since then I've tried to do my duty to my family, my colleagues at work, and to my community." When he died a few weeks later, everyone knew they had known a pillar of strength, one who had by his own life brought power to people.

Another man had finally been forced to commit his daughter to a mental hospital after years of uncertainty and anxiety and several months of acute turmoil and distress for him and his wife. A few days later I drove by his house where he was mowing the lawn. I leaned out the window and said, " Sam, what do you make of it? " He walked slowly over to the car. " All I know," he replied, "is that I'll never say another unkind word about anybody as long as I live."

Strange, isn't it? Out of this kind of suffering there comes strength for living. This is an experience of non-Christians as well as Christians. It is something that men discover about life, just one of the central facts of life, apparently close to its center.

Though Christians have no monopoly on this human experience, they ought to be able to point to something more than the virtues of stoicism. They do, in fact; they point to Jesus of Nazareth. What, then, does all this have to do with Jesus of Nazareth? Just this: his strength came through suffering.

Emily Dickinson put it this way in one of her letters:
"When Jesus tells us about his Father, we distrust him. When
he shows us his home, we turn away. But when he confides to
us that 'he is acquainted with grief' we listen, for that too
is an acquaintance of our own."

So look, then, at "the lonely man of sorrows." What can
be said of him?

The first thing is that he had his measure of success as well
as of failure. The people heard him gladly. They pressed upon
him from every side. He had to struggle at times to hide from
them so he could have some time for himself. Miracles were
performed. His words were listened to. He had a core of
disciples who, when he called them, came.

But he also had his failures. The multitudes who once
flocked to hear him cried for his blood. Those disciples fled
at the end after one had betrayed him. His life ended in failure
in his death on the cross.

Somewhere — we are not sure where — Jesus had come to
accept the fact of his death. By the time he set his face to
go to Jerusalem, he had accepted it. Here the culmination of
his life was to be revealed. Though his friends might consider
Jerusalem to be where he would usher in God's Kingdom and
Israel's enemies be put to flight, it was, in fact, where he would
die and the fulfillment of prophecy was to be expressed. His
entrance into the city was to fulfill the Scripture; and this was
to be done through his suffering and death.

He had been seen as catching up all the threads of the Old
Testament where the pattern of God's plan for the world was
gradually unfolding through his people, and he saw himself
as the instrument of fulfilling them so that God's purpose
might be revealed.

The passion stories in the Gospels draw upon references to
the Old Testament prophecies:

> Rejoice greatly, O daughter of Zion!
>   Shout aloud, O daughter of Jerusalem!
> Lo, your king comes to you;

> triumphant and victorious is he,
> humble and riding on an ass,
> on a colt the foal of an ass.
>
> (Zech. 9:9.)

The Christian church had read the Suffering Servant passages in Isaiah as foretelling in a profound way the passion of Jesus:

> Surely he has borne our griefs
> and carried our sorrows;
> yet we esteemed him stricken,
> smitten by God, and afflicted.
> But he was wounded for our transgressions,
> he was bruised for our iniquities;
> upon him was the chastisement that
> made us whole,
> and with his stripes we are healed.
> All we like sheep have gone astray;
> we have turned every one to his own way;
> and the Lord has laid on him
> the iniquity of us all.
> (Isa. 53:4–6 — part of the whole passage,
> Isa. 52:13 to 53:12.)

The suffering of Jesus, in other words, is seen to be woven into the pattern of Jewish history and reveals itself as the meaning of that history — and so, of the history of all men. The details of the suffering of Jesus are not what is important. It is the fact of his suffering. In some way embedded at the heart of life is this unavoidable fact.

Jesus dealt with it by accepting it as from God, and then offering it back to God. As a result, there was let loose in the world his Spirit to strengthen and comfort men, to bring men together, to reconcile men, men and God. His suffering, in a word, served a purpose — God's. And so with ours.

When we accept the suffering that comes to us as somehow also part of God's plan and offer it back to him, strength is given to people as well as to ourselves. Something happens. Something new takes place. What is an old event — pain —

becomes a new event — strength. What happens always brings power for living and comfort and hope. It lifts people. It reconciles them.

There is, furthermore, a strong relationship between innocency and suffering. The greater the innocence, the greater the power. An old man full of years dies, and though we miss him, we are not greatly moved. But a young child dies — that moves us. In one sharply divided family, a two-year-old grandchild was run over by a drunken driver. Despite the personal antagonisms that had been built up over the years, everyone in that family came to the funeral and to the parents' home afterward. There was mutual forgiveness and reconciliation. One uncle commented, " Little Frances has accomplished more in her two years of life than I have in my forty-five."

When those who knew Jesus of Nazareth looked back after they had seen his suffering, they were able to discern the pattern that God was weaving throughout the history of Israel. When they saw what God did in and through his suffering, then they were able to look ahead with hope and anticipation. God was at work, and he had a purpose. So they could take their suffering in the same spirit.

That is what is happening to us when we suffer. Our response in the same spirit is the heart of our spiritual life.

The last word is that, therefore, *all* things work together for good when we love God — that is, when we trust and obey him. *Nothing* takes place beyond the sphere of God's providence — indeed, of his Kingdom. He is the God of *all* history. Therefore, he is at work in and through all the events of history to bring to fruition the salvation that is implicit in his Kingdom, that is, to bring life and strength to men so they might live as men and know themselves as his children.

This does not mean he causes evil. It does mean that in his created order it is permitted, and indeed it seems at times to be in control. We cannot take with a light spirit Dachau and its evil spirit, or the violence of one race against another, or the ignoring of the poor by the affluent. It does mean, however, that something can be done in opposition to every evil; good can come out of it. God can turn it to good. The way is the only way he works: by the cross. The cross can be borne only by men. So if we are truly men, we can bear our crosses bravely and help him get his way in his world.

XVIII

ON LIFE THROUGH DEATH

There is an advertisement of an English movie (*The Uncle*) that reads: "Every son must forgive his father one thing . . . Gus lost his innocence the summer he was seven-and-a-half when he discovered what it means to be human; when he discovered Sex, Death and Love."

The combination is almost exactly right — Sex, Death, and Love. The only word missing is "Hate." The four together make up the fundamentals of what it is to be a man: there is Love and Hate and there is Sex and Death. In one form or another, one combination or another, they just about sum up the human enterprise — its greatness and its tragedy.

The American people know a good deal about love and sex and hate. If they don't, it's not because our culture has not tried to help them. *Who's Afraid of Virginia Woolf?* is popular, not so much because it teaches us anything, but because it expresses so much of what is hidden beneath the surface of our lives, churning away and bursting into expression only in the dark moments late at night when we drink too much. We don't have to drink too much to know that they are there — the love-hate ambivalences and the drives for sex and power. The advertisement is right. We cross the threshold into adulthood when we are introduced to sex and love and death. Innocency begins to go and maturity begins.

The fact is, however, that there is not much said in our

culture about death. Why is that? Our society tries to cushion death, to hide it, to soften its impact, to pretend it doesn't exist. It doesn't do this with love and sex and hate. They are affirmed. Death, it appears, one wishes could be denied.

Yet it is one of the few facts that can't be denied. It's built right into the system; life begins and it ends. It does this for everyone. There is no escape. Pretending there is never makes it so.

So — what shall we say about death? The first thing to be said is that we might as well accept it, and we might best accept it as the *end*.

Everybody dies. Some die naturally — in the fullness of time, we say — so it is the right time. The fullness of one's life and the completion of it come at the same time. Not many die that way. Some die too late. Their lives have been fulfilled, their minds have gone, their spirits are dead. Only the body goes ticking away until, at last, it comes to a halt.

Most people die too soon and for the wrong reasons — unnaturally: sickness that could not be cured; accidents that should have been avoided. A boat turns over. A tire blows out. An airplane falls. A sniper, mad at the world, kills a President, and another, "born to raise hell," slaughters eight nurses. It's senseless. It's pretty damaging evidence that the whole enterprise is senseless. It shows what *The New York Times*, in commenting on the mass murder from the University of Texas tower, called "the mystery of the defect in humanity."

Strangely, how often we recognize we are the guilty ones when death comes. It is not only that someone who has loved us has died, and we have not been worthy of that love nor responded to it. When President Kennedy died, the nation knew instinctively that it was guilty. We all shared in it. Perhaps this is one reason we try to hide from death: we don't like to acknowledge guilt.

More than guilt (and in part, because of our guilt) we mourn. We mourn not because all those we have known who have died were good men. Some were. Some were not. We mourn because they belonged, somehow, to us. When they died, something in us died, too. That may be another reason we hide from the fact of death. It's all too clear it is coming to us one day.

In any case, whatever death may mean to us, there is one thing certain about what it means to those who have died: life is finished. Sartre says, therefore, any meaning that life has is over, too. So don't bother about putting any interpretation upon life; when it's over, everything — including our thoughts about it — is over. Death cancels life.

We do not have to be too certain about what happens to those who have died. Why this passion for absolute certainty about the character of life after death? Absolute certainty is not a matter of faith. It's a historical, literal, fundamentalist kind of certainty that is so often sought for. But we see through a glass darkly; we walk by faith; and faith is a different matter from absolute certainty. Else why faith?

So let us be this-worldly about death, as this-worldly as we can be. What can we say about our life here and now in the light of the life of those who once were here but are now no longer? If we can come to some understanding of their death, perhaps we can then say something about our life.

The first thing that can be said is this: death brings a depth to life. If someone we love dies, it is just impossible to go on living on the surface of life. That surface is broken, and we look, perhaps for the first time, into the depths that are underneath the surface. There is a new dimension to life, and we can no longer be content with the trivialities. There is a new perspective that causes us to look differently at our family, at our work, at ourself.

When Dean Inge was reflecting about the death of his twelve-year-old daughter, he wrote: "Bereavement is the deepest initiation into the understanding of the mystery of human life, an initiation even more profound than mutual human love." Isn't this a strange observation? We tend (in personal terms) to think that we have found the meaning of life when we are able to love and be loved. He says, No. It is when we love, and then that love is broken — it is then that we are introduced into the most profound understanding of the mystery of the meaning of human life.

It is the same thing that is meant by a young mother, whose two-year-old daughter died, when she says: "After that first ache and pain and emptiness, suddenly one day my life descended onto another level, and my heart keeps singing all the time."

The best hope that any of us can have for people who have been bereaved in the most intimate, personal sense of love that is broken by death is that they may know something of a new depth and perspective to their lives and may have been introduced into a more profound understanding of the mystery of human life. Death brings depth to life.

That is one word that can be said.

There is a second word. It is more difficult to say, and it is more difficult to hear. It is this: We can't try to hold on to those we love who have died. We have to let them go. If we really love them, we have to let them go.

If we try to hold on to them because we miss them, we become consumed with self-pity. The nature of love is not to hold on to another for one's own self; it is to set the other person free to become himself. This is the character even of mutual happy human love at its best: a setting free that a person may, because he is loved, become his best self. Baron von Hügel used to say: "Those you love most you disengage most from yourself."

All love that binds and holds and coerces and refuses to let go destroys and consumes. A parent must set his child free; a couple must be free to choose to love each other every day till death parts them. When death does come, let them go.

It might be helpful to think of this as an offering. They have been given to us — free gifts: love, husbands, wives, children, colleagues, fellow workers, members of a common life. As they have been given to us, let us offer them back.

It is here, if we are Christians, that we offer them back to God. We trust him as the author of all that is good, who has given them to us, and now we offer them back to him. If we are not Christian, we offer them — to what? To whatever understanding we bring to the meaning of life and death and eternity.

The offering, the giving, is the point. It is to remember them before God.

The third word is this: death makes a difference for living. If it makes no difference — if life goes on just the way it has always been — then there is no purpose that can ever be found in the death.

When it is love that is broken, then death always makes a difference. A man can properly say: "I remember when my mother died, and life hasn't been the same since." Or, "I remember when my child died, and life hasn't been the same since." Or, "Since my wife died, my life has moved onto another deeper level." Each successive bereavement can bring greater gentleness, less passion to possess things or prestige or power, an abiding courage, a grounding in life unseen and eternal that cannot be shaken, a willingness not to have your own way all the time, a sense that the men of influence are the men who have suffered, that pain somehow brings greater power than even knowledge, a realization that the deepest satisfactions are in a peace and joy that the world can neither give nor take away, that all life finally is grace.

What a tragedy if the death of someone we love doesn't make a difference so that we can live more fully and deeply than we have ever done before!

What a tragedy if the death of a President doesn't make a difference in our national life! What a victory if his death brings greater life: justice, opportunity, freedom.

But we don't need the tragic drama of assassination to make this point. It is a crystal-clear one: we make of death what we want to.

We cannot be coerced to make one thing of it or another. Nobody — certainly not God — can coerce us. We decide on the basis of our best judgment and faith to make of it what we will.

If death drives us back into life, so much the better. If we become more fully human, then death has served a great purpose. We are made more truly human if we are a little more open to the people around us, if we do the job we are meant to do just a little more efficiently, if we are able to accept the costliness of life as part of the necessary sacrifice we have to make if we are to live wholly. It means, in a word: a little death to the self, or maybe a big one.

If death serves life for us, then we can go on to make one comment about those whose lives are ended. That comment is: life has the last word. By faith that means a new life for those who have died.

We can afford, then, to commit those who have died to their life — their new life — confident that they do live, and get on with our life. Embedded at the heart of life as we see it — and we don't need to trust any life other than the one we know — is a mystery that is illumined by death: the power of atoning love, of offering, of sacrifice, or of costliness — all expressed in the life and death and resurrection of Jesus of Nazareth. That seems to be the closest we can come to knowing the quality of human life at its best. We all can taste that life, for we all shall die.

This hinges, then, upon the phrase above: " all expressed in the life and death and resurrection of Jesus of Nazareth." By this is meant not simply a turning to this historical figure and putting our trust in that historic event back there two thousand years ago. It means a turning to our own experiences of life and death and resurrection and putting our trust in Jesus of Nazareth, acting in them here and now. Or, more accurately perhaps, putting our trust in God, who by his Spirit is carrying out his will in our history today, to affirm the Lordship of Christ — today and forever — this side of the grave and the other side. This affirmation always comes through suffering and death.

In the light of the life, death, and resurrection of Jesus — that is, in the light that comes to our life through faith in him — let us look once again at this relationship of life and death.

In the first place, we see this: God comes to us where he is least expected. We might expect him to come in great power and glory to show his might. But that is not the way he comes. He comes hiddenly. He can't be seen by the naked eye.

The Jews expected him to come as the Messiah who would descend from the clouds and destroy their enemies. He comes instead riding on a donkey, and willing to be destroyed by evil men. Ground is broken for the building of God's Kingdom by digging a hole for a cross to bear a broken body.

Is it not true that this is how God comes to us — not so much in our success as in our failure; not simply when things are going all right, but when things are going all wrong; not only when we are loved, but when we are hated; not only when there is life, but when there is death?

God came in Christ, the least likely person to express his will. God comes into our own life in exactly the same way — where we do not expect him.

That is one mark — the unexpectedness of God. Another is his cost. No cost, no God. The scorn of Bonhoeffer for " cheap grace " is justified. Cheap love that you can buy has no power to move us. To be moved by love, love must cost something. It has to give something up.

God's love cost him his Son. He had to give him up to all the forces of evil. He was willing to pay this cost because this was how God's love for men could be expressed. The cross did not change God's mind; it expressed it.

Thornton Wilder has written: " In love's service only the wounded may serve." Whenever we embrace as well as we can the costliness of love, we take part in the continuing act of redemption of God. We ask him: how will you get your will done in me? He answers: as you are willing to die to getting your own way by obeying me. That's the way of the cross. There is no other way.

This does not explain the origin of suffering and of death. It does, however, affirm that both can serve a purpose. There is a use for them. The purpose is God's. It appears as he is trusted and obeyed and in no other way.

This leads to the third mark — a coming to terms with life that brings a sense of assurance and of being carried by life rather than trying to carry it, being in the mainstream of life. We are "with" it on the deepest level of human existence. Therefore, we can affirm it as good.

The traditional words are peace and joy. Thomas Hooker spoke them on his deathbed when he said: "I am at peace with all men and . . . [God] is at peace with me; and from that blessed assurance I feel that inward joy which this world can neither give nor take from me."

The words may not be contemporary words, but they describe a fact of present human experience: a concrete, historical fact that men know now. You can come to terms with life. You have to come to terms with death first, but once you have done that, life carries you.

So let us turn finally to look at the quality of the resurrection of Jesus Christ. The record of the Gospels is quite clear about the central affirmation: Christ was raised from the dead.

He was raised from the dead and his life begins again. His disciples, who had become frightened and fled — dead spiritually — take on a new life because of his presence. Jesus of Nazareth no longer simply has a message; he *is* the message. He no longer can be thought of as doing special action; he *is* the action. His words no longer simply judge the world; *he* judges it. He no longer simply points to his Father; his Father is *in* him . . . reconciling.

If there is one thing clear about the gospel proclamation, it is that the Christian faith was faith in Jesus of Nazareth, dead and risen. Again, we do not have to be overly concerned about the particular historical events described. They simply reflect the faith in the resurrected Christ. Indeed, the stories of the resurrection differ considerably from one another, but always they are together in pointing to that central resurrection message: Christ is raised! Once this fact had been grasped by the disciples, they then looked back and saw the meaning of all the suffering and the death of Jesus, and they looked forward with confidence because they knew he had triumphed. He is the Lord.

Another way of saying it is that God backed Jesus up. He entered history in him and brings to an end the old world, the old scheme of time, and the old way of victory. That is all connected with sin and death, and it's now done with. What is put in its place now is God's reign, God's Kingdom, everything that Jesus had been talking about. The Kingdom of God has indeed come; it has come not simply in the words Jesus spoke when he walked the earth, in his message, but now his life, death, and resurrection — *he* — have become incorporated in the message. In other words, what is now central is not the teaching of Jesus but Jesus himself. More accurately, Jesus is now central to the message: God's Kingdom has come; Jesus reigns. He is the Lord.

To be sure, this is not visible to the external eye, but to those who believe it in faith, it is this truth which swallows up all lesser truths. In and through life and all the structures of history, Jesus is Lord. This is the faith of the disciples.

Therefore, they move joyfully on, spreading this good news. Though there will be more difficulties, they are carried by joy and peace and hope; their confidence now is in him who is victor over death and Lord of life. The story of the church begins.

XIX

ON "THE DARNED OLD CHURCH"

One reason the church is difficult to talk about is that we generally use interchangeably two concepts of the church which are related to each other but are not the same.

In normal speech, when we speak of the church we think of the Roman Catholic Church, or the Episcopal, or the Lutheran, or whatever. Sometimes we refer to churches within these denominations: St. Cyprian's on Main Street, St. David's on Elm, and St. Paul's on West. These are concrete, visible, historical institutions. We could talk in pretty much the same way about the Republican and Democratic parties and their organizations down to the grass-roots levels.

In ecumenical circles in particular today, we are aware that behind these historic divisions, these institutions that have been (and still are, sometimes) rivals, there is one church. All believers in the God who is revealed in the Son and in the Holy Spirit belong to him and thus to one another. This is a theological way of describing the church, but the historical evidence that this is so is partial and incomplete.

Because Jesus of Nazareth was raised from the dead, the church came into existence by the power of his Spirit. When Peter was trying to describe what was taking place at Pentecost, he said: "This Jesus God raised up, and of that we all are witnesses. Being therefore exalted at the right hand of God, and having received from the Father the promise of the

Holy Spirit, he has poured out this which you see and hear"
(Acts 2:32-33).

Christians are bound, then, by the Spirit to Jesus of Nazareth
in a particular way, in a special community that is God's
people chosen for a special purpose — to proclaim Christ's
Lordship — against which nothing else shall prevail until
the end of time. They belong to God and God belongs to them
in a most special way. Paul says that this community is Christ's
body; everybody who belongs is a member with some special
function to perform, and Christ himself is its head.

In other words, in something of the same way that the words
that Jesus of Nazareth spoke on earth came to be bearers of
him so that he is in and through his words and he *is* the gospel,
or the Word of God, so now he *is* the church. Or, more accurately, it is his Spirit that binds men to him and to one another,
and while they wait his coming again, they worship together,
break bread in his name, pray and affirm their faith in him.

New members are initiated into this community by the
power of that Spirit, through Baptism and the forgiveness of
sins; the work of the community is carried on by all its members, some carrying responsibility for special functions; the
Supper is shared in memory of Christ and in expectation of
his coming; the faith that is the possession of these people is
proclaimed to all men in their life and work in the world.
That faith is that Christ has shown in his death and resurrection the sovereignty of God over every evil power and he
will come again. In the meantime, Christians shall live in this
faith and in trust and in obedience to him.

There is a community of faith in Christ. He — or his Spirit
— dwells in them and they live by his power.

How this community of faith expresses itself changes from
age to age, but the hard core fact of faith — and the faith
relationship — does not change. Jesus of Nazareth is the gospel; he is the Word of God; he is from everlasting to everlasting; he dwells with his people, who confess him in their
worship and show him forth in their lives. The words may

change, but the essential act of trust and hope does not change. Jesus of Nazareth is the heart of it: "You have the words of eternal life; and we have believed, and have come to know, that you are the Holy One of God." (John 6:68-69.)

All of this is by way of background to help us eliminate some of our confusion in talking about the church. One of the difficulties we are faced with in the contemporary world is that we confuse the historical understanding of the church with the theological. We tend to judge the church solely on the basis of its historical record, its successes and failures. If a church becomes integrated, we praise it; and if it remains segregated, we condemn it. Now, these are important features of a church, but they are not all-important. What is equally important is the character and integrity of the church's trust in the Lordship of Christ — is it or is it not a community of faith?

To be sure, "by their fruits ye shall know them" is part and parcel of the gospel. It is a good tree only that brings forth good fruit. The key to that kind of goodness is in the relationship of the members to the head. That is a theological relationship because it rests on trust and obedience.

The Christian faith is a historical faith. It was given once and for all in Jesus of Nazareth, but it is also historical because that faith has to be lived out by people in a historical period in a particular culture. The historical appearance, however, cannot be equated simply with the theological reality.

On the one hand, we take history too seriously, and on the other, we don't take it seriously enough. We take history too seriously when we use history for the purposes of theology. When we look to history for the validation of our faith, we are looking for something history by itself cannot provide. When we look to history for proof of our Christian convictions, we are asking history to do something of which it is not capable.

Our faith cannot be proved. We can't turn to a "Christian" era in history and say that people were more Christian or

happier then than now. Nor can we say that Christian culture
is better than non-Christian, and, therefore, let us be Christians. Our faith is in God — not in history. We put our trust
in the one responsible for history, not in the creatures of history; in him, not his creation.

"Do you believe in the virgin birth?" is the kind of question
that illustrates the confusion. That is a theological question.
It can only be answered theologically — as an act of faith in
Jesus of Nazareth. It cannot be answered with a simply historical "Yes" or "No" answer. "Jesus Christ is the incarnate
Son of God" is a statement of faith and, therefore, on the
same level you can say, "born of the virgin Mary" in a
particular place, at a particular time. Faith, in other words, is
in God's action, not in history, nor in parts of history that we
select because they support our faith.

We have already seen this in dealing with the resurrection
stories. Our faith is not in *them;* it is in *him.* When descriptions of his victory are recorded, they clothe the fact of his
victory. They are not the victory. The historical evidences
point to a theological truth; they are not themselves the truth.
If we ask history to bear the weight and proof of faith, we are
asking it to do more than it can properly be asked to do.

The complementary affirmation, however, must also be
made: We don't take history seriously enough. The Christian
faith *is* historical. Christ did come into history; it is history
that has been redeemed; it is only in concrete historical situations where faith can be lived. Faith, as we know, that does
not "work" is dead. Theological and historical truth are not
separated by the Biblical witness. Rather, the Bible declares
they are bound together.

Therefore, the ethical dimension to *obey* is the dimension
that is so often hard to find when one looks at the church.
Where is the obedience? What are the historical descriptions
of the church that point beyond itself to the Lord of the
church and the world? The point is that you can only obey in
concrete historical situations — right now.

It is wrong to ask the church by her actions to prove the existence of God, but it is not wrong to expect her to give some evidence that she believes in God and is trying to obey him. She should be expected to point to him to give witness to her faith. This should be in how she lives in her life on earth. The world should not be asked to love the church, but she should be given reason to respect her.

So, a young man thinking of the ministry, for example, will ask out loud the question that is on most people's minds: Why worry about "the darned old church"? Does the church have anything constructive to do in society? Is she doing it? What does the church in Selma (or Cambridge), for example, bring to the community of Selma (or Cambridge) by way of reconciliation? Not much. Is the church usually so concerned about herself that she is afraid to act in society? Generally, yes. Does she take any significant leadership in any of the social, economic, political issues? Usually, not. Convention resolutions do not count; actions do. The record of the historical institutional church is not impressive.

Individuals count, of course. Christian members of that community of faith have led marches; they have acted as reconcilers; they have taken positions of leadership in the national life; they try to build bridges. Some have indeed made great sacrifices — even unto martyrdom — in order that they may affirm their understanding of what it means to be men of the twentieth century. It is as citizens, not simply as members of the institution of the church, that they act. In other words, they are worldly in the best sense of the word. That is what Christians are meant to be.

When Peter responded to Jesus in the words quoted above: "You have the words of eternal life; and we have believed, and have come to know, that you are the Holy One of God," he was answering a question Jesus asked, "Will you also go away?" His immediate words were, "Lord, to whom shall we go?"

It is not stretching the meaning of the text too much to ap-

ply it to the church. If we leave the church, then, Lord, where
else shall we go?

There is no other place, not if Jesus of Nazareth is Lord
and the church is his body and we are members of him in it.
Then there is no place to go, not if we are the church. We
cannot jump out of our skins any more than Jesus can leave
his body.

Therefore, no matter what the institutional reasons might be
for leaving the church — ineffectiveness, sin, pride, bigotry,
stuffiness, cowardice — the theological truth is that there is
nowhere else to go. We cannot leave that which we are.

More than that, however, it is through these historical
forms that Jesus continues to come. He does not simply establish the church; he becomes the church. Those who partici-
pate in it belong to him and, therefore, bear him in the world
wherever they go. They may do it well or ill, but they do it
as they must as members of his body.

We are not asked to identify the historical institution in its
explicit activities with Christ (any more than we identify any
particular resurrection story with Christ), but we are asked to
so love that our response through the activities is always a response to him by his Spirit. Then the institution can fall into
its proper place. Our trust does not rest in it; it rests in him.
We can criticize it because we are loyal to him. We can even
oppose it at times because it is he whom we love.

But if we leave it — then to what do we go? There are, I
know, limits set by men which, when overstepped, cause them
to feel that in the name of Christ they must repudiate his
body. Although their courage may be praised and their reasons
understood with sympathy, such a step seems finally in opposition to the faith lived in the New Testament and contrary to
the Spirit of Jesus of Nazareth himself, who never separated
himself from the people of God, Israel, to whom he belonged.

And yet the temptation is great . . .

. . . but to whom shall we go?

One final word. It would be quite easy to urge a young man

to enter the ministry on the grounds that he could lead a very useful life. He could. But that is not the point. The point is: How can he be helped to come to know himself and God and to put his trust in God, and then obey him?

It is the same situation that arises on another level when a person is considering church membership. There may be many very good arguments for becoming a church member, but they are all pointless unless they lead him increasingly to come to know himself and God and to commit himself to God in faith and obedience.

The ministry — to return to the college senior — is a very useful way to spend a life, if he is strong enough. He is immediately put in touch with people and has an opportunity to be a part of and influence their lives as in very few other callings. The so-called failings of the minister are almost always human failings of a person; they are not built in in the structure of the ministry itself. There is no end to the possibilities of good that are within the grasp of intelligent, creative and faithful men.

All this, however, misses the point. It is like telling a minister he can do more good in one place than another. That may be true, but is not sufficient reason for him to go somewhere else. He can go only when he believes that that is what God wants him to do. Those are historical, not theological, arguments, and while they have some bearing on a man's life, they are not fundamental. What is fundamental is his faithfulness to the Lord of life. That Lord comes into the history of a man's life totally at every moment. How he responds to *him* — either toward the ministry or away — is all that matters.

It is that response to Jesus of Nazareth in and through the situation of the immediate moment which is the heart of the Christian life for all men — not just ministers. It is *at once* a response to Jesus and to men, to the church and to the world.

The young man asking the questions about the ministry of the church is no more than every Christian asking the identical questions about his membership in the church. The ordination of the layman takes place at his Baptism; his essential life in Christ is not different from that of any priest. His ministry may be exercised in a different way, according to his work in the world, but the nature of his life in Christ is the same. His response to Jesus of Nazareth in his own situation is the same heart of the Christian life. It is at one and the same time a response to Jesus and to men, to the church and to the world.

XX

ON GOOD TIMES IN THE NEXT–TO–LAST TIMES

We live in a day when the spiritual life can be understood and lived only as human life. This means a life which is both personal and social. The personal develops out of the social. The formation of a man's personality, and therefore of his spirit, is developed within the structure of his family, his community, his school, and all other social organizations of which he is a part. He develops his individual style.

Therefore, any understanding of this kind of formation is spiritual understanding. How the family exists, how it regards itself, what it is to be a member of a particular family, what the interpersonal relations are within the family, all make up the raw material out of which a man's spirit is fashioned. The insights of depth psychology, then, are obvious spiritual insights insofar as they lead to self-understanding and, therefore, to maturity and a sense of individual worth and freedom.

To become familiar with the thought of men who give us this kind of understanding of man is not only a proper but an essential spiritual exercise. Indeed, such men as Freud, Jung, and Rank are, in fact, spiritual leaders, and the more they can be recognized as such, the greater the possibility that they may be used for the spiritual — that is, human — work of Christ and his church.

After all, it is through self-understanding that we come to some understanding of others, and through understanding others that we come to better self-understanding; and the quality of these relationships determines, in large measure, our understanding of God. Is he friend or foe? Well, our personality structures help us decide. This is how God comes to us, so we had better understand the make-up of ourselves as well as we can. The more that love can hold together all personal relations, the more we shall know of the love of God.

It is in and through the structures of society that the spirit of that society is formed and justice is made more or less possible for greater numbers of people. These structures are political, economic, and social. They are concerned with everything that affects society from population control and poverty programs to rehabilitation of cities, from black power and white power struggles to the state of the theater and arts, from the regulation of fair trade practices and collective bargaining to the casting of votes for surrogate judges and for presidents. There is nothing in society that does not have its bearing on the welfare of the people — their human welfare, that is to say, their spiritual welfare.

To talk of the spiritual life, therefore, as though these concrete facts of life did not exist — and, indeed, as though they were not the most important (bread and butter) facts for most people — is sheer blindness. The spiritual man is the political, economic, and social man because he is a human being.

Therefore, knowledge of these structures of society — how they work, how they can be changed, how they make a more just society — is spiritual knowledge. Men and societies are formed by them, and anyone who takes the spiritual life seriously is called to take these structures seriously. It is within these structures — right here and now — that the Kingdom of God is coming to pass and being expressed. A repudiation of the importance of these structures is, in fact, a repudiation of the structure of the Kingdom of God. Each step toward a more just society in any area of its life is a spiritual step.

Spirituality, therefore, cannot be anything but a man's total life. The life of the Spirit has to be rooted and grounded in the soil of human life: eating, drinking, earning a living, doing military service, making love, laughing at jokes, popping beer can tops on a picnic, paying for the beer, getting in and out of debt, passing out hand bills for favorite candidates, burying the dead, tossing little children into the air, listening to Negroes talk about their fears, and (sometimes) their fears overcome. The spirit of man springs from this human ground; nothing human is foreign to it.

So spirituality is grounded in the human situation. But it is also a good deal more than that. It deals with the human question, " What is man? " and asks with the psalmist, " that thou art mindful of others? " It is the human situation in relation to Jesus of Nazareth and his Spirit. Christian spirituality is the merging of the human spirit with his Spirit and together creating new men and new societies, giving expression visibly to the hidden Kingdom of God that is in our midst.

That is why we have tried to concentrate on those issues of life or death or failure or success or whatever which arise naturally out of ordinary human situations and to try to discern how the Spirit of Jesus is already at work in those situations. He is there. His Spirit is there. He is to be responded to right there through those human experiences and structures of society in faith and obedience. That is Christian spirituality.

This means combining our understanding of the concrete human situation with our understanding of Jesus of Nazareth and of what God has done in him and is doing in us by his Spirit. This is done by reflection, understanding, prayer, and commitment to that Spirit in decision and action. The total response is the spiritual life. It is a total response because there is no separation between what we do, on the one hand, in response to men and, on the other, in response to God. The response is to man and society and to God at one and the same time.

The situation, then — the situation together with the Spirit of Christ — determines what the response will be. Situations differ and change. Therefore, the responses will be different and change. What is right here may be wrong there; and what is God's will today may need to be expressed in a different way tomorrow. What does remain constant is the fundamental act of allegiance to God and obedience to him in accordance with the Spirit of Christ as that is understood at this time in this situation.

This does not mean a capricious and individualistic understanding and action. The individual member belongs to a corporate body, the church, and when he acts, he does so only as a member of that body. There will be differences of opinion among those members as to what Christ, the Head, wants by way of response — the more of this the better, for only so can the understanding of the meaning of changing human situations move the church along with changing society, but always within fundamental loyalty to him.

The church is the people of God — all the people of God. The significant mark is the sign of the cross in Baptism, when a Christian name is given which separates men from other men who are not given such a name. They are separated, however, so that all men may know their true nature. This can be done only as those given a Christian name move with them into the world, doing their jobs alongside them, carrying on the world's work as well as they can, to help them see where Christ is at work and to see why Christians say the world is Christ's. Baptism does not make Christians superior to other men. It makes it possible to serve them.

All this has to do with the mission of the church and the ministry of the laity. The words are not important — certainly not to twentieth-century man. But what they represent is important: who is man and what is he doing here? This participation in the life of men in the world is the only way Christians can bring their answers for consideration by contemporary men. If Christians are not involved with modern men on the terms set by modern men, how can they be heard?

This, of course, blurs the distinction between clergy and laity as being the essential distinction, and rightly so. They

are one in Christ. That is their essential nature, and it is one
of unity, not division. Distinction, yes, but distinction of function rather than essential being. All men go about their life's
work in Christ, some doing one thing, others another. Some
are dentists and bartenders; others are priests and religious;
some are activists, others are contemplatives; some are servers,
others wait.

When the Kingdom of God is fully revealed, we shall see
that the " last things " incorporate and fulfill all the " next to
last things " with which we have been concerned in life — all
the historical clothing we have had to wear, like being born in
a certain family in a certain year, in a specific country with a
specific color to our skin, belonging to a particular nation with
definite causes, clubs, and churches. The partial life of all these
historical institutions or particularities will then be revealed as
they really are in God's Kingdom and in the light of Christ's
coming again.

In the meantime we wait — wait and work. We do so as
people and communities and churches pointing toward the last
things. It falls upon us, therefore, to see that there is embodied
in our historical clothing all that is necessary to remind men
" between the times " of what the " last times " shall be like
when all life shall be clothed in the glory of the Almighty.

Take monastic communities as an illustration. The life of
the religious — their spirit and their *raison d'être* — is part of
this total life in God, and their witness, therefore, is as important as any witness of any member of Christ's body meant to
show forth the glory of God. They are as much a sign of God's
Kingdom as the most active marchers on picket lines. They
both are the church. Neither one alone is. Together they point
to our partial incompleteness in history and beyond themselves to the fulfillment of our particularities in God's Kingdom in his time.

The form of these religious communities will change. They
always have. But their spirit — Christ's Spirit in them — will
not change. That is the same, and its work is to draw men

closer together in brotherly love, to open themselves to others and to the society of which they are a part, to keep their attention focused on Christ and his Spirit in their common human life, to trust him, to wait, and to obey.

It is exactly the same as the spiritual life of all Christian men. The expression of that spirit changes, but how else is Christ to bring his Kingdom to pass except through the members of his body, each in his appointed way? The religious communities have always an " eschatological witness " to make first and then a practical witness — just like the church itself.

This is no different from what all Christian institutions will be doing in the twentieth century. The more the better, and, probably, the sooner the better: religious orders, theological seminaries, parish churches, liturgical rites and forms of worship, diocesan and other conventions, and all the present historical and institutional forms that the church has to do Christ's work. These institutions are simply the historical forms; there is nothing sacred about them. Our faith is not in them. Our faith is in Christ.

His Spirit will continue to feed us in the breaking of bread. Indeed, it is in that central act of the sacramental life where we meet Jesus of Nazareth and feed upon him, that we shall be given eyes of faith to see him more clearly feeding us in every act within his created universe. To see Christ more and more in his secular order does not mean we see him less and less in his sacramental order; nor to live with him amongst the people of the world to repudiate him amongst his Christian people. The deeper we go into the sacred, the farther we can go into the secular, until at last we see that both are joined together by his grace, which is everywhere.

This means to go deeply within ourselves. Enough has been said to make it clear that the way to holiness is, as Hammarskjöld says, the way to action. But this does not mean a repudiation of that interior life, " the dumb region of the heart," where we live with our faiths and fears, our decisions and indecisions — and with Christ.

It is his Spirit that dwells within us. We are baptized in that Spirit. In him *is* our life. Just as the spirit of a man passes into the life of his wife or neighbor — or whomever he loves — so does the Spirit of Jesus of Nazareth pass into our lives. He loves us as mortal man loves — and how much more! He who came to dwell with us and give his life for us dwells now with us in his Spirit with a divine love.

When we think about our life, therefore, in the light of that Spirit; when we ponder what the things of this world mean in relation to that Spirit; when we use our best judgment to figure how we can relate our ways to his way — then we are praying. It is the response of *all* we have — mind, body, spirit — to him.

It is incorporating all that we *are* — our heritage that has formed us, our society that has molded us, our loves and hates that have left their marks upon us — as well as all that we *do* — our decisions and actions in life — and in response to him who dwells in our heart, in the life of the world, and in all eternity. This is prayer — this total response to God.

Is not our life hid with Christ in God? Well, then, in that hiddenness, in the deepest depths of our being, let us talk, look, listen, wait, be drawn up, possessed, incorporated, contemplate, hide, adore him whose judgment and salvation come to bring new life and make us new creatures. He is all in all. We are hid with him in his creation in the world and in his redemption. Let us therefore wait upon him, rest in him, indeed, be him and affirm him. For it is not we but Christ who dwells in us, who works and wills his good pleasure.

This is no naturalistic flight of the alone to the alone. It is the living in the Spirit — within the Spirit — who comes to us only through others and our common world and the stuff of life. We live in that Spirit as we trust him and obey him in that complex, varied expression of himself through those others and their spirit and still within us in our interior spirit. Let us not, therefore, sharpen too greatly the distinction between ourselves, other selves, and God. They are all mixed together in that common membership in a common body with many different members and one Head.

We are free, then, to seek our way — each within the common life and responsible to one another — as God himself leads us. The " instructions " in the spiritual life are given to those who belong to one another in his Spirit. They are given interiorly and always in relation to the exterior relationships. Will you teach us to pray, then? " Say, *Our* Father . . . : *He* will teach you."